香港歷史考察之旅
Hong Kong History Excursion

新界區及離島
New Territories and Outlying Islands

鄭寶鴻 著
Cheng Po Hung

商務印書館

香港歷史考察之旅：新界區及離島

作　者：鄭寶鴻
前言翻譯：張宇程
責任編輯：張宇程
美術設計：趙穎珊
出　版：商務印書館（香港）有限公司
香港筲箕灣耀興道 3 號東滙廣場 8 樓
http://www.commercialpress.com.hk
發　行：香港聯合書刊物流有限公司
香港新界荃灣德士古道 220-248 號荃灣工業中心 16 樓
印　刷：美雅印刷製本有限公司
九龍觀塘榮業街 6 號海濱工業大廈 4 樓 A 室
版　次：2020 年 12 月第 1 版第 1 次印刷

ISBN 978 962 07 5866 9
Printed in Hong Kong

Hong Kong History Excursion: New Territories and Outlying Islands

Author: Cheng Po Hung
Translator to introduction: Chris Cheung
Executive editor: Chris Cheung
Art design: Cathy Chiu
Publisher: The Commercial Press (H.K.) Ltd.,
8/F, Eastern Central Plaza, 3 Yiu Hing Road, Shau Kei Wan, Hong Kong
http://www.commercialpress.com.hk
Distributor: The SUP Publishing Logistics (H.K.) Ltd.,
16/F, Tsuen Wan Industrial Centre, 220-248 Texaco Road, Tsuen Wan, Hong Kong
Printer: Elegance Printing & Book Binding Co., Ltd.
Block A, 4/F, Hoi Bun Industrial Building, 6 Wing Yip Street, Kwun Tong, Hong Kong

First edition, First printing, December 2020
ISBN 978 962 07 5866 9
Printed in Hong Kong

Contents

序
Preface iii

路線一 新界區廣域遊
Route 1 Tour of the Extensive Area of New Territories 2

路線二 火車行大運之旅
Route 2 New Territories Train Roundtrip 22

路線三 新界巴士遊
Route 3 New Territories Bus Tour 40

路線四 沙田懷舊遊
Route 4 Nostaglic Tour on Sha Tin 58

路線五 大埔探索遊
Route 5 Discovery Tour on Tai Po 90

路線六 新界北區發展遊（粉嶺、上水、沙頭角及羅湖）
Route 6 Tour on the Development of the North District (Fanling, Sheung Shui, Sha Tau Kok and Lo Wu) ... 112

路線七 元朗及屯門發展之旅
Route 7 Tour on the Development of Yuen Long and Tuen Mun 142

路線八 荃灣、葵青及馬灣現代化之旅
Route 8 Tour on the Modernization of Tsuen Wan, Kwai Tsing and Ma Wan 208

路線九 離島環迴遊
Route 9 Roundtrip on Outlying Islands 242

路線十 隱世迷人景點遊
Route 10 Tour on the Hidden Attractions 280

參考資料
Reference 296

鳴謝
Acknowledgement 296

序

2000 年，香港大學通識教育部主管陳載澧教授賜電約見在下，討論由我來講述有關「昔日香港」之講座的可行性，並輔以三次包括港島中西區、東區以及九龍區街道和名所舊蹟的考察之旅，並着我設計步行路線。

當時，我正在編寫由三聯書店出版的有關港島、九龍及新界街道系列拙著，故有不少可供參考的現成材料。

就在與陳教授會面的數天後，我將構思好的步行路線大綱，連同「昔日香港」之講座內容，以及大量可用作今昔對照的早期照片呈交陳教授省覽，幸運地旋即獲知照准實行。

在講座開展同時，亦蒙香港大學美術館邀約，舉行多個不同主題的演講，介紹早期香港社會面貌。因此，大學通識教育部的考察之旅中除學生外，亦有部分博物館人員及聽眾出席。

這次考察之旅所涉及的範疇，包括香港、九龍歷次填海、海岸線遷移、銀行、金融、娛樂、宗教、醫療、教育、新聞、軍事地帶、警政、天氣、飲食、工商業以至建築物等項目，題材亦算廣泛，因而有戰戰兢兢的感覺。

及至 2003 年至 2004 年，香港大學美術博物館將我於該館演講之部分內容，輯錄出版了《香江知味》、《香江風月》及《香江道貌》一共三本書，內容分別是有關香港早期飲食、娼妓和電車路風光，每次出版皆會舉辦展覽。同時，該館的博物館學會，亦要求我舉辦一次從石塘咀至筲箕灣的電車遊，逐一介紹拙著述及之景點及其他名所舊蹟。

兩年後，北京中央電視台來港拍攝《香港名街》特輯，亦邀請我作了一次電車遊，以及一次以中西區大小街道為主題的步行考察。2015 年，中央電視台又邀請我拍攝有關 1941 年至 1945 年香港淪陷期間的特輯，當中談及被改作日化名稱之的街道，以及曾更改用途的建築物，包括被改作「香港佔領地總督部」的滙豐銀行大廈、被改作「憲兵隊本部」的現終審法院，及依次被改作「日軍指揮部」及「東亞酒店」的半島酒店等。他們亦專程前往拍攝被改作「豐國印刷工場」之商務印書館及其龐大廠房之北角原址。

較具特色的一次，是陳載澧教授着我陪同他以及由台灣來港的著名作家陳映真先生，進行一次中上環區考察，講述百多年來香港的華洋金融業，以及銀行業發展。

由2001年開始，賞面邀約在下舉辦步行考察以及電車遊和巴士遊的單位，包括公營部門、博物館和學術機構；有一次香港電台電視部亦隨團拍攝。

另一次具特色之懷舊遊，是步行中上環多條街道，懷緬百多年來的報館和印務館，還有皇后大道中及利源東街等早期報紙集散中心。出席者為籌辦中之香港新聞博覽館的多位骨幹成員，包括慕名已久的陳淑薇女士、陳早標先生等。

我亦十分高興目睹該博覽館於2018年12月5日，在原必列啫士街街市落成開幕，開始為市民服務。

過去十多年，考察之旅曾步行經過具特別主題和風格的街道里巷，包括銀行區的皇后大道中和德輔道中；華人金融和貿易區的文咸東、西街；刻製圖章的文華里；別名「花布街」的永安街；娼院區的水坑口街；塘西風月區的皇后大道西及山道；西洋紅燈區的春園街和駱克道等。

在九龍半島則包括尖沙咀九龍倉（海港城）；水警總部所在的麥當奴道（後易名廣東道）；兩旁榕樹密佈、早期被形容為「恍如鬼域」的羅便臣道（後易名彌敦道）；「蔴埭（油麻地）花國（娼院區）」的吳松街和廟街；還有早期為海旁馬路主要街道之差館街（即上海街）等多條街道。此外，亦包括九龍城及寨城區的大小街道。

至於途徑的港九早期名所舊蹟，則有銀行金融機構、百貨店舖、工展場地、馬場、遊樂場、戲院、茶樓酒家、西餐食肆及茶餐廳、酒店、纜車、電車、火車和巴士總站、碼頭、船塢、貨倉、公用事業機構、工廠、街市、辦館、廟宇、教堂、學校，還有填海區和機場。

▲ 筆者在2001年九龍考察遊之後，與香港大學學生在中環蓮香樓品茗，位於筆者（正中）右鄰的是陳載灃教授。

多年來，在下亦常經乘搭火車或巴士前往新界旅行、郊遊、野餐、探親，以及新春「行大運」。火車沿途所經的地區有大圍、沙田、馬料水（現大學站）、大埔、粉嶺、上水及羅湖等。

而巴士途經的主要路線青山公路，所經的地區則有葵涌、荃灣、深井、青山酒店、容龍別墅、青山寺、青山灣、元朗、新田及錦田等。

對於上述新界區的街道及名勝，在下仍有深刻印象及美好回憶。

現將往昔在港九市區之考察遊覽路線，以及所經歷之旅行、郊遊經驗，作一綜合性之分區分段逐一介紹，並配以歷史圖片及相關說明，冀能從另一角度呈現香港早期面貌，期望與有心人士一同走入時光隧道，進一步探索香港早期歷史。

路線一

新界區廣域遊

Route 1

Tour of the Extensive Area of New Territories

前言

1861年，英國人根據《北京條約》，接管現界限街以南的地區，名為英屬九龍。而位於界限街以北仍為中國管轄的地區，則名為華界九龍或中國九龍，亦有稱為新安縣者。當時華界九龍亦包括大部分離島。

1870至1880年代，報章亦不時出現深圳上水鄉、新安縣新田村、新安長洲，以及新安縣屬大嶼山等地名。

當時，新界（華界九龍）居民主要集中於元朗、錦田、屯門、大埔、沙田，以及離島的大嶼山、南丫島和長洲等地，以農耕及捕魚為主，亦有從事製鹽、造莞香及燒灰等業務。

不同村落的村民，多為自給自足。因交通不方便，九龍市區是遙遠的地方，甚至鄉村與鄉村之間，不少村民都是因關山阻隔而「老死不相往來」者。

早期新界的道路，大部分為高山及平原之間連接多座鄉鎮的羊腸小徑，最寬只為五英尺，一條往來元朗與荃灣之間、在山段興築的元荃古道現仍保留。

以下為十九世紀後期報章上一些中國九龍和英屬九龍與港島關係的報導。

1874年4月，一宗發生於華界深水埔（埗）垃圾灣（醉酒灣）的背夫賣子、將所得以貼姘夫的案件，原夫往英界九龍的油蔴地差館報案。稍後，亦有不法之徒在英屬九龍犯案而潛逃往中國九龍轄下的深水埔（埗）之新聞。

急（汲）水門（馬灣）以及將軍澳之佛頭洲，設有釐金廠（稅關），駐有中國兵勇。稅關船隻皆有旗號。稅關接受船隻報稅，抽取釐金及緝私。此外，亦有釐金廠位於長洲、橫欄島、九龍寨城、深水埔（埗）及荔枝角。因香港乃免稅港，大量船隻在此活動。

1884年3月，新安長洲闔境，在報章刊登長洲廟宇及玄天上帝（北帝）太平清醮啟事，由西營盤鹹魚欄店號代收善信捐款。北帝廟建於乾隆四十八年（1783年）。

同年9月，九龍城約內有2,000名華兵駐守，恐法國人乘中國士兵防守鬆懈而潛入。當時，九龍城賭館林立，華差置之不理。

1885年10月3日，中國礦務總局就開採新安縣屬大嶼山鉛鑛山之礦場招股，由港島之安泰公司辦理。

1895年5月，一名東涌居民在沙螺灣倒

斃，東華醫院獲得通知，該院即通知有關親屬往東涌守府衙門查問。

同時，一艘九龍稅關之小艇，在筲箕灣海面被英警拘查，控其越界，因證據不足而獲釋。

1898年6月9日，中英在北京簽訂《展拓香港界址專條》，租借由現界限街以北迄至深圳灣和大鵬灣的華界九龍地段，連同界內的大小海域以及多個大小島嶼，為期99年，直到1997年6月30日為止。俟後，華界九龍改名為「新界」，而深水埔（埗）、荔枝角、九龍城、鯉魚門以至將軍澳一帶則劃入市區，定名為「新九龍」。

英國於1899年4月接管後，將新界劃分為包括九龍、沙頭角、元朗、雙魚、六約、東海、東島洞及西島洞等8個全約，屬下有41個分約。荃灣及沙田隸屬於九龍全約，大埔、粉嶺及上水隸屬於雙魚全約，屯門及大欖涌則隸屬於元朗全約。東島洞全約屬下則有吉澳、東平洲及塔門等，西島洞全約則有大嶼山、長洲、坪洲、馬灣、赤鱲角及青衣等島嶼。

1900年，當局將8個全約改劃為16個約。英國接管新界後，宣佈所有土地為官地，原居民擁有永久業權的「紅契」改為期限只到1997年6月30日的官契。新界居民感到不滿及無奈。

1901年，有7,000餘畝的新界土地種植甘蔗，而荃灣一帶的不少土地則種植菠蘿，不時引致瘧疾。當時在荃灣亦有一間菠蘿廠，大部分農地則為稻田。

1911年，港督盧吉（Frederick John Dealtry Lugard）宣佈，平（屏）山、凹頭、上水、沙頭角、大埔、沙田、全（荃）灣等警署，兼辦生死人口之註冊。又在淺（荃）灣、長洲及大澳等警署審理小額錢債案。當時，部分新界警署亦兼辦郵政業務。

新界農村於農曆正月十五上元節，各戶皆張燈結綵，於去年誕下男丁的居民，會把書有男孩及父親姓名的花燈，懸掛於祠堂或神廟內。

1926年，新界鄉議局成立，是民意機構和官民溝通橋樑。

1950年代，新界多區不時於晚上10時起至凌晨6時實施宵禁，各大墟市均嚴格執行。

五、六十年代，新界農耕的稻穀分有水稻、鹹水稻及旱稻，而稻米則有花腰子、齊眉、絲眉及黃粘等，年產約50萬擔（一擔為100市斤）。1969年稻穀豐收，農田間呈現一片金黃色。

早於1950年代，不少稻田被改作魚塘。到了1970年代，不少稻田改為種植蔬菜、水果及花卉。

1969年，新界共有2,200畝魚塘，大部分位於元朗，主要出產品種為烏頭、鯇魚及鯉魚。

由1960年代後期起，當局陸續在新界各區發展新市鎮。到了1980年代中，共開闢了6,000公頃土地，並在大埔、元朗及將軍澳興建工業邨。

1980年，當局計劃發展大嶼山，打算興建跨海大橋連接青衣、馬灣及大嶼山，並在赤鱲角興建新機場。此「玫瑰園計劃」於1989年實行。新機場於1998年啟用。

早於1960年代起，當局陸續興建多條連接港島、九龍迄至新界、途經多條隧道及大橋的幹線，當中包括獅子山隧道、屯門公路等。而由西九龍快速公路經葵涌、汀九橋、大欖隧道至元朗的三號幹線，以及來往新機場的青嶼幹線等，對促進新界及大嶼山的發展，居功至偉。

Introduction

In 1861, the British took over the area south of Boundary Street under the *Convention of Peking*. The area was called British Kowloon. The area north of Boundary Street was still under Chinese control, and was called Chinese Kowloon, or San On County. At that time, most of the outlying islands were included in Chinese Kowloon.

In the 1870's and 1880's, names of places like Shenzhen Sheung Shui Heung, San On County San Tin Village, San On Cheung Chau, and San On County Lantau Island often appeared on the newspapers.

Then, people living in the New Territories (Chinese Kowloon) distributed mainly in Yuen Long, Kam Tin, Tai Po, Sha Tin, as well as outlying islands including Lantau Island, Lamma Island and Cheung Chau. They made a living by farming and fishing. Some also engaged in manufacturing salt, incense sticks, and burning ashes.

Most of the villagers were self-contained. The Kowloon urban district and other villages seemed too far away to them due to a lack of transportation. They seldom met other people other than those in their own village.

In the early days, most of the roads in New Territories were just winding trails connecting different villages between mountains and valleys. The widest one was only five feet. Yuen Tsuen Ancient Trail, which was built on the mountain, connecting Yuen Long and Tsuen Wan, is still in place.

The followings are some news about Chinese Kowloon, British Kowloon and their connections with the Hong Kong Island in the late nineteenth century.

In April 1874, a woman betrayed her family in Sham Shui Po in Chinese Kowloon. Her husband reported the case to Yau Ma Tei Police Station in British Kowloon. Later, a case in which someone broke the law in British Kowloon and then fleed to Sham Shui Po in Chinese Kowloon was reported on the newspaper.

Customs offices stationed with Chinese soldiers were located at Kap Shui Mun(Ma Wan) and Junk Island in Tseung Kwan O. There were flags hanging on every customs vessel. Tax declaration, tax paying and anti-smuggling were all conducted by the customs. Customs offices were also found in Cheung Chau, Waglan Island, Kowloon Walled City, Sham Shui Po and Lai Chi Kok. A lot of vessels often gathered around the customs offices since Hong Kong was a duty-free port.

In March 1884, a notice about Pak Tai Temple (built in 1783 during the Qing Dynasty) and the Cheung Chau Da Jiu Festival was posted on the newspaper. The worshippers' donation was then collected by the salted fish shops in Sai Ying Pun on the Hong Kong Island.

In September 1884, there were approximately 2,000 Chinese soldiers stationed in Kowloon City to prevent the French from sneaking in. Lots of gaming houses situated there were left unchecked by the Chinese policemen.

On 3 October 1885, the Chinese authority issued shares to raise fund for lead ore mining on Lantau Island in San On County. On Tai Company on Hong Kong Island acted as the guarantor.

In May 1895, a resident of Tung Chung was found dead in Sha Lo Wan. Tung Wah Hospital informed the bereaved relatives to visit the "yamen" (government office) in Tung Chung for enquiry.

At the same time, a Kowloon customs vessel was arrested by the British police in Shau Kei Wan for crossing the boundary, but was later released due to insufficient evidence.

On 9 June 1898, China and Britain signed the *Convention Between Great Britain and China Respecting an Extension of Hong Kong Territory*, in which the territory in Chinese Kowloon from the north of Boundary Street to Shenzhen Bay and Mirs Bay, as well as the maritime spaces and outlying islands within were all leased to Britain for 99 years with an expiry day on 30 June 1997. Later, Chinese Kowloon was renamed the "New Territories". Sham Shui Po, Lai Chi Kok, Kowloon City, Lei Yue Mun and Tseung Kwan O were included in the new urban area known as "New Kowloon".

After the British took over the New Territories in April 1899, the territories were divided into eight sections (known as "yeuk" in Chinese), including Kowloon, Sha Tau Kok, Yuen Long, Sheung Yue, Luk Yeuk, Dong Hoi, Dong

Dou Dong and Sai Dou Dong. There were also 41 subsections under these eight sections. Tsuen Wan and Sha Tin were put under Kowloon section. Tai Po, Fanling and Sheung Shui were put under Sheung Yue section. Tuen Mun and Tai Lam Chung were put under Yuen Long section. Kat O, Tung Ping Chau and Tap Mun were put under Dong Dou Dong section. Lantau Island, Cheung Chau, Peng Chau, Ma Wan, Chek Lap Kok and Tsing Yi were put under Sai Dou Dong section.

In 1900, the eight sections were rearranged into 16 sections by the authority. All land in the New Territories was turned into crown land and the "red deeds" which represented the perpetual ownership of the indigenous inhabitants were converted into crown deed which expired on 30 June 1997. The inhabitants were discontented with the change.

In 1901, around 7,000 acres of land in the New Territories was used to grow sugar canes. And some of the land in Tsuen Wan was used to grow pineapples, which often lead to malaria in the nearby area. At that time, there is a pineapple factory in Tsuen Wan, while most of the farmland was rice fields.

In 1911, Governor Lugard announced that birth and death registration were also handled in police stations in Ping Shan, Au Tau, Sheung Shui, Sha Tau Kok, Tai Po, Sha Tin and Tsuen Wan. Small claims cases were handled in the police stations in Tsuen Wan, Cheung Chau and Tai O. Postal services were also provided in some police stations in the New Territories.

Villages in the New Territories would often hang lanterns and other decorations on the fifteenth day of the lunar new year. Families that had new born son in the previous year would hang lanterns in the ancestral hall or temple, with names of father and son written on the lanterns.

In 1926, Heung Yee Kuk, an advisory body, was established as a communication channel between the authority and the inhabitants in the New Territories.

In the 1950's, curfew was often imposed between 10pm and 6am in various districts in the New Territories.

In the 1950's and 1960's, various types of rice were grown in the New Territories, and the annual output was around 500,000 piculs (1 picul equals to 100 catties). During good harvest period in 1969, the field displayed a gold color.

As early as the 1950's, some of the rice fields were turned into fish ponds. In the 1970's, rice fields were converted into fields that grew vegetables, fruits and flowers.

In 1969, there were 2,200 fish ponds in the New Territories, mostly situated in Yuen Long. Flathead mullet, tench and carp were the major produce.

From the late 1960's, the authority began to establish new towns in various districts in the New Territories. In the mid 1980's, 6,000 acres of land had already been developed. Industrial estates were set up in Tai Po, Yuen Long and Tseung Kwan O.

In 1980, the plan to develop Lantau Island included building a cross-harbour bridge connecting Tsing Yi, Ma Wan and Lantau Island, as well as a new international airport at Chek Lap Kok. The "Hong Kong Airport Core Programme", commonly known as the "Rose Garden Programme", commenced in 1989. The new airport was put in use in 1998.

From the 1960's, several new routes, tunnels, and bridges connecting Hong Kong Island, Kowloon and New Territories were built one after the other, including Lion Rock Tunnel and Tuen Mun Road. Route no. 3 which travels from the West Kowloon Highway, via Kwai Chung, Ting Kau Bridge, Tai Lam Tunnel to Yuen Long, and Lantau Link which travels to and from the new airport contribute much to the development of the New Territories and Lantau Island respectively.

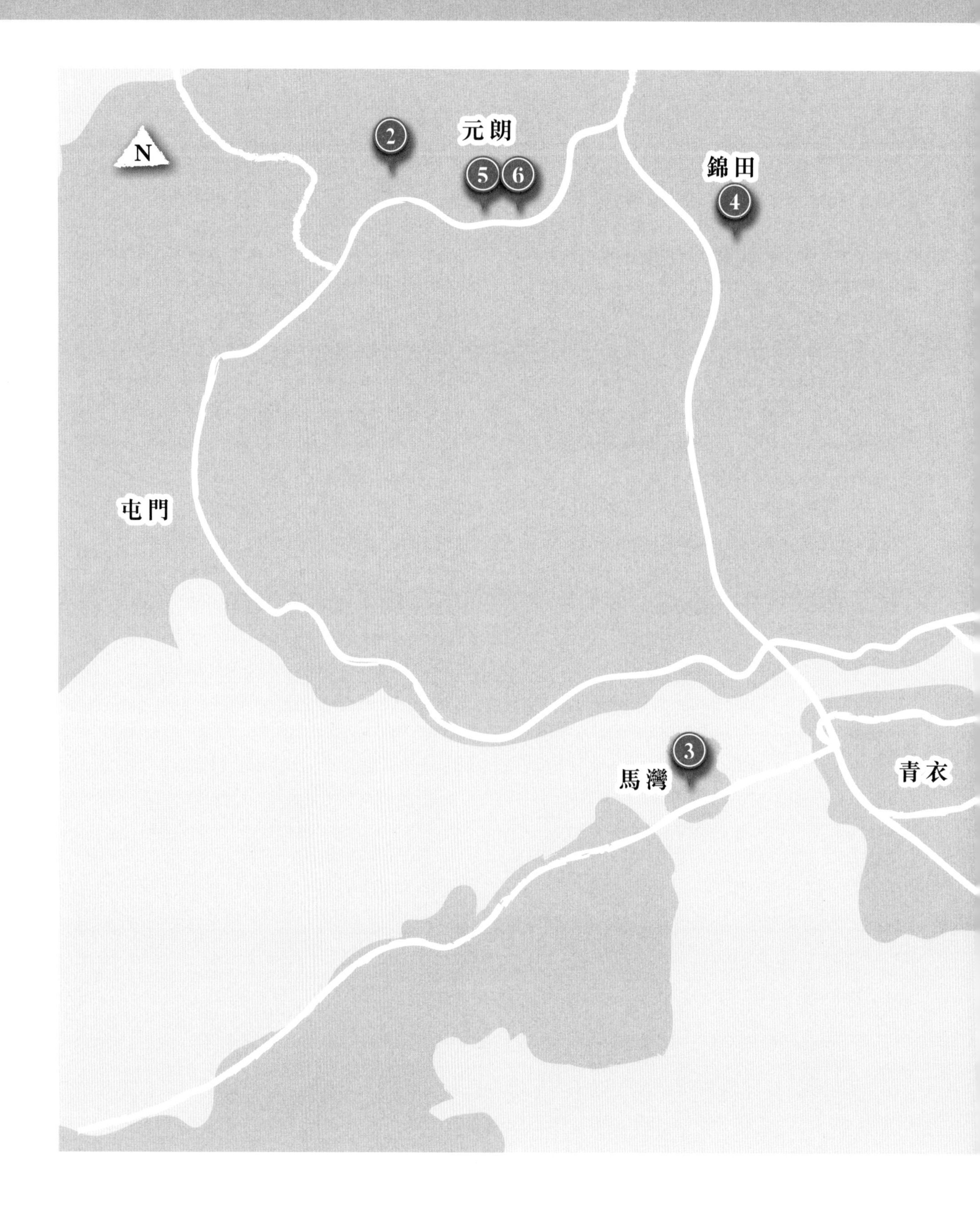
N
元朗
2
5
6
錦田
4
屯門
3
馬灣
青衣

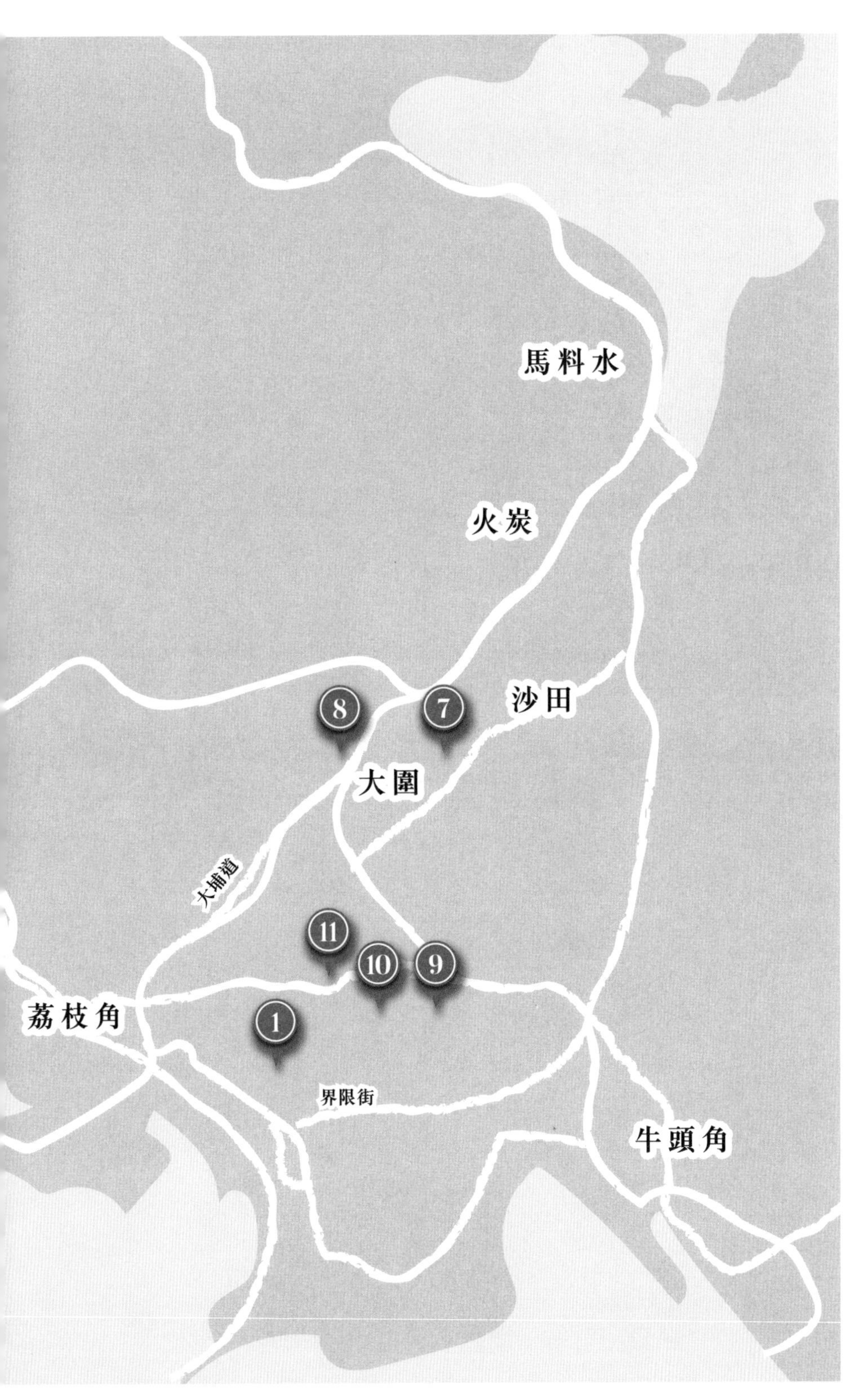

Please scan the below QR code for English map.

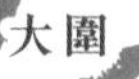

① 1898年，位於中國九龍（新界）的中國軍警與英國官員。

The Chinese soldiers, policemen and the British officials in Chinese Kowloon (New Territories), 1898.

約 1899 年英國接管新界前，位於元朗屏山的一家糧油雜貨店。

A provision and oil stall in Ping Shan, Yuen Long at about the time of the lease of New Territories, 1899.

沙田

大圍

約 1900 年的馬灣。

右方為天后廟。左方為興建於 1868 年的中國海關，當時已改為警署。

Ma Wan, c. 1900. The Tin Hau Temple is on the right. The police station (former Chinese Customs) is on the left.

位於錦田接近吉慶圍的永隆圍，約 1930 年。

Wing Lung Wai, near Kat Hing Wai, Kam Tin c. 1930.

約 1899 年，新界農村的原住民。

The inhabitants of a village in the New Territories, c. 1899.

新界元朗一帶的居民和遊客，約 1900 年。

Villagers and tourists in Yuen Long, New Territories, c. 1900.

4
5 | 6

沙田大圍一帶，約 1920 年。

左方可見獅子山。正中是九廣鐵路的路軌。

Tai Wai, Sha Tin, c. 1920. The Lion Rock is on the left. The track of Kowloon Canton Railway is at the centre.

經過近沙田大埔道的運乾草客家婦女，約 1928 年。

Hakka women, delivering straw, passing along Tai Po Road near Sha Tin, c. 1928.

華界九龍（新界）的九龍城區內的九龍灣，約 1900 年。

這一帶於 1930 年代發展為啟德機場。右方為飛鵝山。

Kowloon Bay of Kowloon City District in Chinese Kowloon (New Territories), c. 1900. The area was developed into Kai Tak Airport in the 1930's. Kowloon Peak is on the right.

7
8 | 9

華界九龍區內的石板橋，約 1900 年。

圖中可見一名肩挑農作物的農民。

A peasant carrying agricultural produce on a stone bridge in Chinese Kowloon, c.1900.

約 1900 年的華界九龍（新界）。

圖中正在開闢道路。

Road construction in Chinese Kowloon, c.1900.

路線二

火車行大運之旅

Route 2

New Territories Train Roundtrip

前言

和平後，很多市民於週末及假期，尤其是農曆年假期間，租用汽車或乘坐火車及巴士，環繞新界一周，稱為「行大運」。他們亦會選擇在若干景點停駐瀏覽、遊玩和品嚐新界特色美食。

熱門的起步點是大圍車公廟。相傳車公曾驅趕沙田的疫症，故該廟向來香火鼎盛，尤其是農曆正月初三適逢赤口不宜拜年，眾多市民到此參拜求籤，並一轉風車，以求好運。七、八十年代，大圍以雞粥馳名。繁忙的沙田站四周則有多個景點，學生旅行團多往參觀道風山和萬佛寺，該寺前有由利園山移至的觀音像。之後，多會前往隔田村的紅梅谷野餐或燒烤，食材及烹調用品則購自火車站對面的沙田墟。

在五十年代初填海而闢成的沙田墟，內有一間沙田戲院，以及楓林小館、三紅花園酒家及牛奶公司餐室等多間酒家及食肆。六、七十年代還有一艘「沙田畫舫」海鮮艇。

沿火車路軌一直走約 20 分鐘，可抵達在 1938 年開業、位於下禾輋以乳鴿馳名的龍華酒店，以及充滿商業氣氛和「遊樂場化」的西林寺。該一帶亦以山水豆腐馳名。龍華酒店的「雀局菜」和供觀賞的白孔雀皆吸引不少遊人和孩童。1965 年，龍華的美味燒乳鴿分為細、中、大三種，價格分別為 2 、3 、4 港元。

五、六十年代，晨曦或薄霧中的沙田，景色迷人，引來大批沙龍拍友和攝影名家到此獵影「攞景」。

每逢週末及假期，大量遊人會在何東樓碼頭和馬料水站（1969 年易名為大學站）前，乘街渡或小輪前往塔門、東平洲或吉澳等離島旅行；亦有不少年輕人乘船前往馬鞍山烏溪沙青年新村的渡假營。旅遊人士也愛往附近大埔滘區的「松仔園」，取道步行前往城門水塘等各區的遠足點。

馬料水站附近的熱點首推充滿詩意的雍雅山房，遊人可在此飽覽吐露港的湖光山色，尤其受情侶歡迎。

當時，大埔區亦有不少旅遊景點，包括位於雲山山腳的松園仙館，內設園林酒家、石舫餐廳，亦有遊樂場提供電影、粵劇及機動遊戲等節目。偶爾，筆者會在廣福道及附近的酒家食肆用膳。

其他遊覽區還有放馬莆林村的天后廟和許願樹、嘉道理農場、梧桐寨的林村飛瀑；最刺激的是沿仙姑峰登上八仙嶺，欣賞大埔周圍的自然景色。近年的新景點則為大埔墟舊火車站的鐵路博物館。

粉嶺的著名景點為供奉呂祖的道觀蓬瀛仙館，其宏偉的大殿以及若干座於園林佈局內的亭台樓閣，皆值得欣賞。

七十年代，筆者喜歡在上水的內街漫步，尤其在街市旁的石湖墟舊街、新豐路及巡撫街一帶進餐，以及購買土特產。六、七十年代見到的兩間金舖——四喜及南盛現時已面貌一新。

羅湖火車站是連接內地的車站，在1980年之前是香港人來往內地所必經者，自內地實施改革開放後，羅湖橋粵港以及車站兩邊地段的發展，可以用翻天覆地、一日千里來形容。

Introduction

After World War II, many Hong Kong citizens used to travel by car or train to go for a round trip within the New Territories during weekends or pubic holidays, especially the Lunar New Year holiday. They would choose to stop over at certain attractions for sight-seeing and enjoy the special cuisines.

Che Kung Temple in Tai Wai was a popular starting point. It is said that Che Kung had helped drive out the pandemic in Sha Tin, so the temple was crowded with worshippers, especially during the third day of the lunar new year. On that day, people would worship Che Kung, draw fortune sticks and turn the windmill inside the temple. There were a number of attractions near the Sha Tin Railway Station, for example Tao Fung Shan and Ten Thousand Buddhas Monastery, both were popular destinations for school tour. People would also go picnic or barbecue in Hung Mui Kuk, and the food and utensils were usually brought from the Sha Tin Hui (Market) opposite the railway station.

Sha Tin Hui was built on the reclaimed land in the 1950's. There was a theatre, and some famous restaurants. In the 1960's and 1970's, there was also a Sha Tin Floating Restaurant.

Walking along the rail track for 20 minutes, one would reach Lung Wah Hotel in Ha Wo Che, which was opened in 1938 and famous for its fried pigeons. The commercialized Sai Lam Temple was also nearby. The area was well-known for its bean curd. The cuisines and the white peacock in Lung Wah Hotel attracted lots of visitors of all ages.

In the 1950's and 1960's, the beautiful scenery of Sha Tin attracted lots of people to shoot pictures there.

During weekends and public holidays, visitors would take a ferry or a small vessel at Ho Tung Lau Pier and in front of Ma Liu Shui Railway Station (renamed as University Station in 1969) to Tap Mun, Tung Ping Chau or Kat O. Some young people would travel to the campsite of the Wu Kai Sha Youth Village in Ma On Shan. Travellers would also visit Tsung Tsai Yuen in Tai Po Kau, and go hiking near Shing Mun Reservoir.

The most famous attraction near Ma Liu Shui Railway Station was Yucca de Lac, where visitors could enjoy the astonishing scenic view of Tolo Harbour down the hill.

There were also a lot of attractions in Tai Po, for example, Green Ville Amusement Park at the foot of Wan Shan, where one could find restaurants, cinema, Chinese opera theatre and other gaming facilities. I would sometimes visit the restaurants on Kwong Fuk Road and nearby.

Other attractions in Tai Po included the Tin Hau Temple and Wishing Trees in Fong Ma Po Village of Lam Tsuen, Kadoorie Farm, and Ng Tung Chai Waterfall. The most exciting experience was to go up Pat Sin Leng (literally means "Ridge of the Eight Immortals") via Hsien Ku Fung and to have a spectacular view of the natural scenery around Tai Po. Recent attraction includes the Hong Kong Railway Museum converted from the past Tai Po Market Railway Station.

Fung Ying Seen Koon, a Taoist temple, was a famous tourist spot in Fanling. Its huge main hall and the pavilions within the garden are worth visiting.

In the 1970's, I would stroll on some small avenues in Sheung Shui, and have meals at the restaurants on Shek Wu Hui Old Street near the market, San Fung Avenue and Tsun Fu Street. I would also purchase some local specialties there. See Hay Jewellery and Nam Shing Goldsmith which were operated in the 1960's and 1970's have taken a completely new look nowadays.

Lo Wu Railway Station, connecting the mainland, was the only station Hong Kong people go to and return from the mainland before the 1980's. Since the implementation of the Economic Reform and Open Door Policy in the mainland, development on both sides of Lo Wu Bridge was said to be revolutionized.

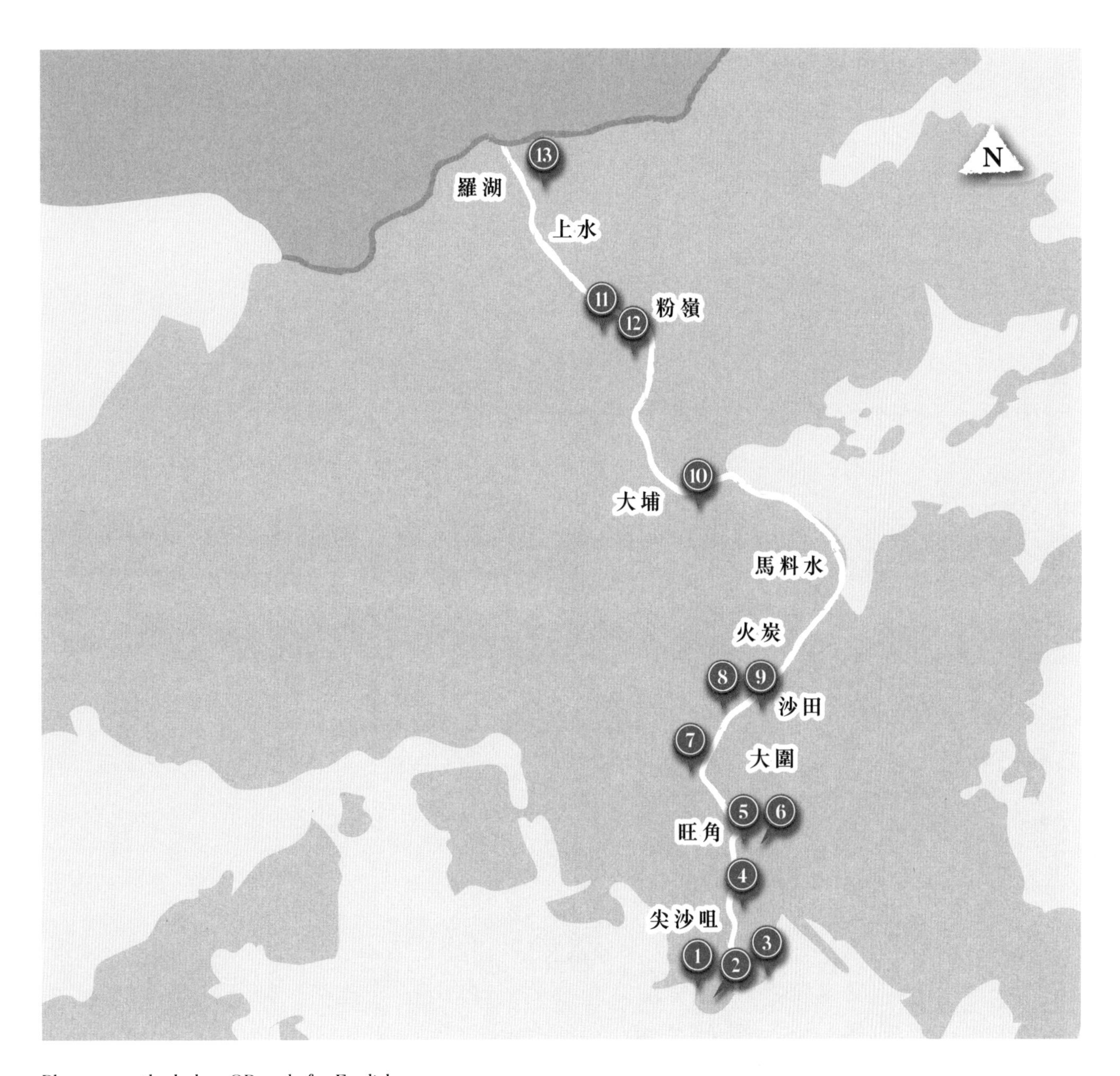

Please scan the below QR code for English map.

53

① 位於尖沙咀的九廣鐵路總站，1973年。

前方可見一部柴油火車頭。在對岸的港島可見於同年落成的康樂（怡和）大廈。

A diesel train in front of the Kowloon Canton Railway Terminal at Tsim Sha Tsui, 1973. The Connaught Centre (Jardine House) can be seen on Hong Kong Island.

鐵路總站內的情景，約 1925 年。

左方為站長室。右中部為三等票售票處。因未到售票時刻，賣票處仍關閉。此現象一直維持到 1960 年代。

Station master's office (left) and third-class ticket booth (middle right) inside the Kowloon Canton Railway Terminal, c. 1925.

紅磡火車站及列車，約 1915 年。

紅磡站因設施殘舊於 1921 年被裁撤。

A train at Hung Hom Station, c. 1915. The station was cancelled in 1921 due to its dilapidated state.

4 因旺角火車站重建而臨時設置的車站，1981 年。

（圖片由何其銳先生提供）

The temporary Mong Kok Station, 1981.

九龍塘站及電氣化列車，約 1983 年。

An electric train at Kowloon Tong Station, c. 1983.

兩名在列車上售賣小食的小販，約 1965 年。

Two hawkers selling snacks inside a third-class train compartment, c. 1965.

正進行闢建九廣鐵路的開山及舖設路軌工程，1909 年 4 月。

估計工地為煙墩山隧道位於沙田的入口。

Cutting and track-bed construction in progress, probably at the Sha Tin entrance of the Beacon Hill tunnel, April 1909.

沙田

大圍

正靠近沙田站的列車及貨卡，約 1949 年。

A train and the cargoes approaching Sha Tin Station, c. 1949.

沙田站的乘客和郊遊人士，約 1950 年。

（圖片由梁紹桔先生提供）

Passengers and travellers in front of Sha Tin Station, c. 1950.

沙田

大圍

停泊於大埔墟站的一列客貨火車卡，1930 年代。

站牌的左方可見古典的候車亭。

A train and the cargoes at Tai Po Market Station, 1930's.

粉嶺火車站的英軍，1920 年代。

（圖片由香港歷史博物館提供）

The British military at Fanling Station, 1920's.

粉嶺火車站，約 1915 年。

此站亦為前往沙頭角的窄軌小火車支線的終站。圖中左方為龍躍頭，右方為軍地。

The terminus of the Sha Tau Kok Branch Railway at Fanling Railway Station, c. 1915. Lung Yuek Tau (left) and Kwan Tei (right) can be seen beside the railway part of Fanling.

沙田

大圍

羅湖火車站及列車，約 1975 年。

此為九廣鐵路英段的終點站。

Lo Wu Station, the terminus of the Kowloon Canton Railway (British section), c. 1975.

路線三

新界巴士遊

Route 3

New Territories Bus Tour

前言

五、六十年代，新界遊所乘搭的交通工具，主要包括由佐敦道碼頭開出，經沙田、大埔、粉嶺、上水至文錦渡的15號線巴士；由佐敦道碼頭開出，經荃灣、深井、屯門至元朗的16號線巴士，還有由元朗開出，經凹頭、米埔、落馬洲、金錢村至上水的17號線巴士。到了1960年代後期，增加了一條由佐敦道碼頭開出，經大帽山荃錦公路至元朗的68號線巴士。

巴士遊的熱門景點，是早期名為「勒馬洲」的落馬洲，不時會碰上大批外籍遊客。在那兒可瞭望深圳河兩岸以及深圳區一望無際的農田。1970年代，落馬洲公廁曾獲全香港「最乾淨和衛生公廁」之美譽。

接着是位於新田區大生圍的泰園漁村。該龐大的遊樂場式漁村，可供垂釣，亦有筵開數十席的宴飲酒家，其附近亦有生生漁村及泰和漁村。這一帶現時是別墅屋苑錦繡花園所在。

必看的景點為「歷史城堡」錦田吉慶圍，以及用鐵環連結製成，曾被英軍於1899年攻佔新界時當作戰利品的一道鐵門。

位於元朗屏山、約於1486年落成的聚星樓，是一座六角形的三層古塔，又名「文塔」或「魁星塔」。聚星樓連同新田的大夫第及青松觀，曾於1980年被政府取材印製一套特種郵票，因而廣受市民留意。

位於元朗舊墟錦田河邊的魚塘南生圍，長堤垂柳，一如江南水鄉，1950年代已有眾多攝影家在此取景。筆者曾由南生圍作起點，途經天水圍、輞井圍等多個漁塘，以及一座玄關帝廟，最後抵達尖鼻咀和流浮山。

在流浮山，可見設於后海灣的蠔田，遊人多在此品嚐美味的即開生蠔。六、七十年代，筆者多在一間裕和塘酒家大快朵頤，亦在此採購蠔油、蠔豉和本地蔬菜；也不時在元朗大馬路的榮華酒家或龍城酒家午膳。

沿着青山公路往屯門，在兩旁可見一列尤加利樹。屯門的著名景點為歷史悠久的青山禪院，內裏有青雲觀、杯渡庵及韋馱殿等建築。在下面一座大牌坊上，有1920年代港督金文泰爵士(Sir Cecil Clementi)的「香海名山」題字。六十年代，筆者曾在禪院旁的大涼棚內享用齋菜。在此亦可觀賞青山灣的日落景色。

始建於1949年的青松觀亦為遊覽勝地。中國大殿式的道觀配合一座壯觀之牌坊，加上眾多不同形態的盆栽，景色相當吸引。

曾有一座鹿苑酒店位於現新墟街市旁，著名景色包括一水榭、九曲橋和一湖心亭，吸引不少遊客。酒店約於 1980 年被拆卸，所在現時有一條鹿苑街。

另一著名別墅為位於青山道（公路）十九咪、具園林之勝的容龍別墅。因可供泊車，遊客喜在其附設的酒家進餐。而其對出的青山灣海面，亦有一艘美侖美奐的太白海鮮舫。此外，附近的三聖邨一帶，還有多間酒家食肆，提供生猛海鮮，吸引不少「識食」的市區客。部分容龍別墅的建築物於 1980 年代後期改建為屋苑容龍居。

可與容龍別墅互相輝映的，乃同以園林花木取勝、位於青山道（公路）十七咪的青山酒店。其廣大庭園內設有中西食肆、茶座及兒童遊樂場，可供遊客及兒童留連較長時間。多套電影亦曾在此取景。

位於青山公路深井段，有大企業生力啤酒廠及嘉頓麵包廠。到 1980 年代，啤酒廠不時安排市民及學生參觀，於 1990 年代，啤酒廠房被改建為住宅屋苑碧堤半島。1970 年代初，筆者不時在深井村登上蓮花山，往大欖涌一帶遠足，之後多在深井的街檔式食肆品嚐出爐燒鵝。

1960 年代，位於汀九、青山道（公路）十一咪半的麗都灣，吸引不少市區的弄潮兒。該處水清沙幼，確為一游泳勝地。筆者當時曾光顧一間名為「麗海」的泳屋。

五、六十年代，最熱門的學校旅行遠足景點，包括荃灣老圍的東普陀佛寺、圓玄學院和三疊潭，尤以東普陀佛寺所陳列的佛教文物甚有觀賞價值。當時是由中環統一碼頭乘小輪，先經青衣上落客再往荃灣，然後步行登上半山的各處名勝。

時至今天，荃灣區的矚目景點，是由古老屋村變身為民俗博物館的三棟屋博物館，以及原海壩村所在的德華公園。

六、七十年代，仍有多間紡織、製衣、醬油調味品及涼果等的廠房，位於荃灣至葵涌之間的一段青山公路，當中包括東亞太平及南豐紡織廠、南海紗廠、同珍及羅三記醬園，以及任合興果子廠等。現時全被改建為包括工廠大廈等的新式建築物。

瞬間，美孚新邨在望，已抵達巴士遊尾站荔園遊樂場。至此，「行大運」的旅程亦告圓滿結束。

Introduction

In the 1950's and 1960's, major transportations to the New Territories included bus route no. 15, which travelled from Jordan Road Ferry Pier, via Sha Tin, Tai Po, Fanling, Sheung Shui to Man Kam To; bus route no. 16, which also travelled from Jordan Road Ferry Pier, via Tsuen Wan, Sham Tseng, Tuen Mun to Yuen Long; and bus route no. 17, which travelled from Yuen Long, via Au Tau, Mai Po, Lok Ma Chau, Kam Tsin Village to Sheung Shui. In the late 1960's, there was a new bus route no. 68, which travelled from Jordan Road Ferry Pier, via Route Twisk to Yuen Long.

Famous attraction of the bus tour was Lok Ma Chau, which was often crowded with foreigners. Visitors could view the riversides of the Shenzhen River and the farmland in Shenzhen district from Lok Ma Chau. The public lavatory in Lok Ma Chau had been praised as the "cleanest and most hygienic lavatory in Hong Kong" back in the 1970's.

Another attraction was Tai Yuen Fishery Garden in Tai Sang Wai. The huge fishery garden offered different kinds of recreation facilities, for example fishing, and had a Chinese restaurant that could cater for large banquets. Sang Sang Fishery Garden and Tai Wo Fishery Garden were nearby. The area was later transformed into a residential estate, Fairview Park.

The must visit attractions were Kat Hing Wai, a Punti wall village in Kam Tin and the gates made of iron rings, which were taken as a trophy by the British army when the New Territories was occupied in 1899.

The three-storey, hexagonal Tsui Sing Lau Pagoda (built in 1486) in Ping Shan, Yuen Long was another worth visiting attraction. The pagoda, together with Tai Fu Tai Mansion in San Tin and Ching Chung Koon (Taoist temple) had drawn the public attention since they were used as the theme of a set of special stamps.

Nam Sang Wai (fish pond), which situated on the riversides of Kam Tin in Yuen Long Kau Hui, was famous for its beautiful scenery that resembles the water towns in Jiangnan in China. In the 1950's, a lot of photographers would go there for shooting. I would start my journey at Nam Sang Wai, via some fish ponds in Tin Shui Wai and Mong Tseng Wai, and Yuen Kwan Emperor

Temple and finally arrive at Tsim Bei Tusi and Lau Fau Shan.

In Lau Fau Shan, visitors could see the oyster farms at Hau Hoi Wan (Deep Bay) and also taste the delicious fresh oysters there. In the 1960's and 1970's, I used to dine in Yu Wo Tong Restaurant nearby and would purchase some local specialties including oyster sauce, dried oysters and vegetables. I would often have lunch in Wing Wah Restaurant or Lung Shing Restaurant on Castle Peak Road in Yuen Long.

Eucalyptus trees were planted on both sides of the Castle Peak Road towards Tuen Mun. The famous attraction in Tuen Mun was the historical Tsing Shan Monastery, in which there were Tsing Wan Kwun, Pui To Hut, and Skanda Hall. There is a memorial archway under the monastery with inscription by Governor Clementi. In the 1960's, I had had a vegetarian dish near the monastery. Visitors could also see the beautiful sunset at Castle Peak Bay.

Ching Chung Koon, which was built in 1949, was another tourist spot. The Taoist temple, in concert with an archway and different kinds of plotted plants, offered an attractive view.

There was a Luk Yuen Hotel near the market in San Hui in Tuen Mun, which attracted many visitors. The hotel was demolished in 1980 and Luk Yuen Street is now in place.

Another famous hotel in Tuen Mun was Dragon Inn, situated at 19th mile of Castle Peak Road. Parking lots were provided in the hotel so many tourists would choose to dine in the restaurant there. Tai Pak Floating Restaurant was situated at Castle Peak Bay outside the hotel. There were also several Chinese restaurants near Sam Shing Village, providing fresh seafood to urban visitors. Part of the Dragon Inn was converted into Dragon Inn Court in the late 1980's.

Castle Peak Hotel, situated at 17th mile of Castle Peak Road, was comparable to Dragon Inn. The hotel had different types of restaurants, a tearoom and a children's playground for visitors to spend their leisure. Several movies were also shot there.

San Miguel Brewery and Garden Bakery were then located on Castle Peak Road in Sham

Tseng. In the 1980's, the brewery often arranged visits for local citizens and students. In the 1990's, the brewery was demolished and a residential estate, the Bellagio, was built on the site. I used to travel to Lin Fa Shan from Sham Tseng Village and go hiking in Tai Lam Chung, and often ended the journey with a delicious roasted goose at the food stalls in Sham Tseng.

In the 1960's, Lido Beach at 11.5th mile of Castle Peak Road near Ting Kau was a famous swimming spot for urban visitors. The beach, with clear water and fine sand, was perfect for water sports. I had patronized a swimming house called "Lai Hoi" there.

In the 1950's and 1960's, famous attractions for school tour included Tung Po Tor Temple in Lo Wai, Tsuen Wan, Yuen Yuen Institute and Sam Dip Tam. The Buddhist cultural relics displayed in Tung Po Tor Temple were quite worth seeing. In those days, people would first take a ferry at the United Pier in Central, via Tsing Yi to Tsuen Wan, and then walk up the mountain to visit the attractions.

Nowadays, tourist attractions in Tsuen Wan include Sam Tung Uk Museum, which was converted from a historical village, and Jockey Club Tak Wah Park, the original site of Hoi Pa Village.

In the 1960's and 1970's, there were still several manufacturing plants of textile, clothing, condiment, and preserved fruit industries on Castle Peak Road between Tsuen Wan and Kwai Chung. They included Nan Fung Textiles, South Sea Textiles, Tung Chun Soy Company, Lo Sam Kee Soy Company and Yam Hop Hing Preserved Fruits Factory. The factories were all converted into modern industrial buildings later.

In the blink of an eye, we arrive at Mei Foo Sun Chuen, and reach the final stop at the Lai Chi Kok Amusement Park. The bus tour also ends here.

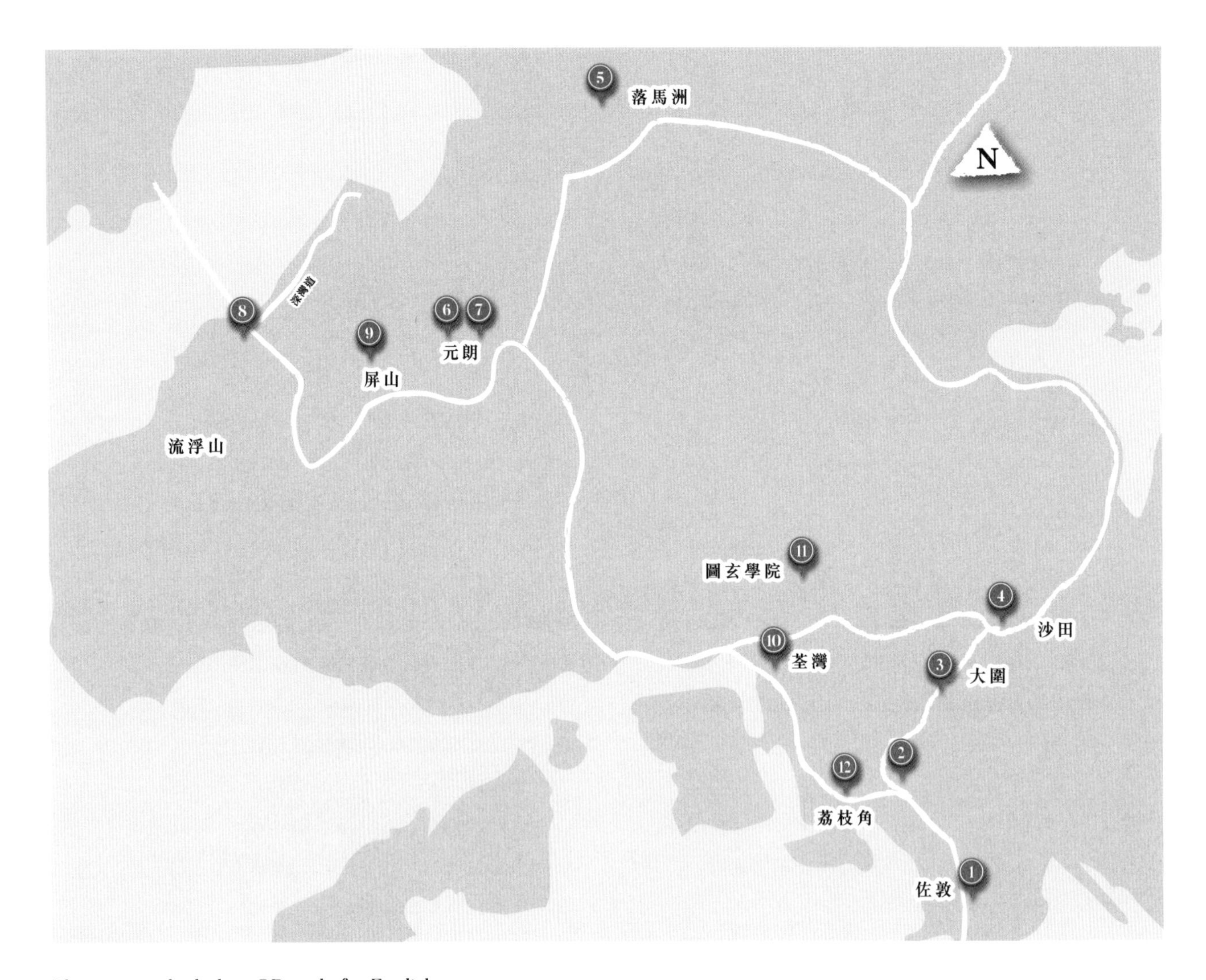

Please scan the below QR code for English map.

沙田
大圍

一輛行駛佐敦道至元朗的 16 號線改裝巴士，正經過彌敦道與加士居道交界，約 1950 年。

戰後因巴士嚴重不足，不少貨車改裝為巴士。改裝巴士車尾為普慶戲院。港九的改裝巴士同於 1951 年後消失。

After World War II, numerous trucks served jointly with Kowloon Motor Bus Company in providing public transport service. The one in the picture is a truck-converted route no. 16 bus, travelling between Jordan Road and Yuen Long, which is passing through Nathan Road near Gascoigne Road, c. 1950.

Coca-Cola
7up
利民士多
永安堂
7up

前往沙田及大埔等地的巴士路線，途中經過大埔道（公路）上的華爾登酒店，約 1960 年。

該酒店可眺望長沙灣一帶景致，在五、六十年代頗為著名。所在現為屋苑爾登豪庭。

The Carlton Hotel on Tai Po Road, an important route between Kowloon and the New Territories, c. 1960. The hotel, where the residential estate Monte Carlton is situated today, was famous for a spectacular view that overlooked Cheung Sha Wan area.

大埔道上另一間知名酒店——接近大圍的沙田大酒店，約 1962 年。

因可供泊車，不少人會在酒店餐廳進食。

Another hotel near Tai Wai on Tai Po Road, Sha Tin Hotel, with a famous restaurant, c. 1962.

約 1960 年的沙田大埔道（公路）。

左方為火車站。右方為沙田墟及巴士總站。

Tai Po Road, Sha Tin, c. 1960. Sha Tin Railway Station is on the left. Sha Tin Hui and bus terminus are on the right.

2 | 3
4

位於落馬洲邊境禁區道路的出入口，約 1965 年。

正中欄閘的背後為華界。

Lok Ma Chau, c. 1965. The area behind the fence lies within the Border Closed Area.

沙田

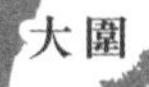

元朗大馬路（青山道），約 1960 年。

圖中多幢三層高樓宇現仍保留。左中部為巴士總站。圖右的龍城大酒家旁為谷亭街。

A bus terminus on Castle Peak Road, Yuen Long, c. 1960. Kuk Ting Street is on the right.

牆紙
裝修
傢俬
公司
十八鄉

沙田

大圍

元朗阜財街的節慶醮會舞龍盛況，約 1980 年。

Traditional festival dragon dance on Fau Tsoi Street, Yuen Long, c. 1980.

元朗流浮山，約 1965 年。

右方為深灣路的巴士站。其上為警署。正中為以生蠔馳譽的裕和塘酒家，是遊客必到的食肆。

Lau Fau Shan, Yuen Long, c. 1965. A police station and a bus stop on Deep Bay Road are on the right. Yu Wo Tong Restaurant, famous for oysters, is at the centre.

沙田
大圍

9 屏山一帶及青山道（公路），約 1948 年。

當時道路仍為單線雙程對頭行車，後來才逐漸擴闊。兩旁遍植尤加利樹。

Narrow Castle Peak Road, near Ping Shan, with Eucalyptus trees planted on both sides, c. 1948.

10 荃灣眾安街，約 1969 年。

可見一輛前往荃灣碼頭的巴士。當時仍有渡海小輪由中環前往荃灣，中途停靠青衣島。

A bus heading to Tsuen Wan Ferry Pier on Chung On Street, Tsuen Wan, c. 1969.

位於荃灣三疊潭的道觀圓玄學院，約 1965 年。

五、六十年代，該處為學校熱門旅行目的地。1970 年代，若干齣古裝電視劇集曾在此取景。

The Yuen Yuen Institute in Sam Dip Tam and Lo Wai, Tsuen Wan, c. 1965. The Institute was a famous scenic spot in the 1950's and 1960's.

沙田

大圍

約 1968 年的荔枝角區。

圖中可見於同年落成、部分為荔枝角大橋的葵涌道。前方為同一時期落成的美孚新邨部分期數樓宇。此為巴士遊終點站。

Lai Chi Kok district, c. 1968. The road at the centre with a bridge on top is the just completed Kwai Chung Road. Mei Foo Sun Chuen is at the front. It is the final stop of the bus tour.

路線四

沙田懷舊遊

Route 4

Nostalgic Tour on Sha Tin

前言

環繞新界一周「行大運」的第一個景點是沙田。

沙田原稱為瀝源，區內有積存圍（大圍）、火炭及馬料水等；亦有煙墩山（筆架山）、獅子山和大老山等若干座山峰。1899 年，沙田被編為隸屬於九龍全約，而相隔一個沙田海的馬鞍山，因地理上位於西貢半島，被編為隸屬於東海全約。

早期，由沙田前往九龍，需攀過現沙田坳道一帶的山段往九龍城，「與世隔絕」，困阻重重。1902 年，大埔道（公路）築成後，鄉民方能步行前往，或用手推車將農作物運往深水埗及油麻地等區。1910 年，九廣鐵路通車後，由新界往來九龍的交通進一步改善。

1911 年 3 月，香港飛船（飛機）會（Hong Kong Aircraft Club）在沙田村（現瀝源一帶）進行飛機演放，經歷數日失敗，終於在 3 月 27 日成功飛上 60 英尺上空。

由當時直到 1950 年代，沙田仍以農耕為主。和平後，當局在火車站對開一帶進行填海，以闢建沙田墟。1950 年已完成一半。同年，為慶祝車公廟重修 60 週年，舉行萬緣勝會，追悼先靈。

1952 年，沙田墟全部落成，墟內設有一個街市及一間配種豬合作社，當局亦於同年在此舉辦農展會。稍後，一間沙田戲院以及多間食肆在此開設，當中包括楓林小館、三紅花園酒家及牛奶公司餐室等。當年，每週約有 5,000 名港九市民到沙田「旅行」，參觀望夫山、道風山、萬佛寺及西林寺等名勝。一年前，即 1951 年在該區增設大圍火車站。

同時，有不少來自內地的「過氣」文武大官，在沙田火車站之上的半山定居，過着農牧生活。

1955 年 11 月，沙田十年一度之建醮盛會開壇，儀式包括恭迎車公進壇，由大埔理民府官身穿漢服長袍馬褂主持開燈禮，大量市區市民到此參觀。

同年，在馬料水增建一個火車站，以配合同年由堅道遷至的崇基學院。1969 年該站易名大學站，同年香港中文大學遷入。

1958 年，馬料水小輪碼頭啟用。3 月 22 日，位於馬鞍山的烏溪沙兒童新村開幕，為當時世界最大的孤兒院。於 1970 年代初，筆者不時在馬料水乘船前往塔門、東平洲以至吉澳等島嶼遊覽。

1962 年，颶風「溫黛」襲港，沙田為重災區，多人傷亡。

1967 年及 1978 年，兩條由九龍塘至沙田的獅子山隧道先後通車，使由市區往新界的交通大為方便。

1969 年，政府決定將沙田發展為新城市，在該區興建多個住宅屋邨，並築建新馬場，後者於 1978 年 10 月 7 日啟用。

1976 年，在沙田「填田」而興建的首個公共屋邨瀝源邨落成。

1985 年，沙田至上水之幹線吐露港公路通車。

1986 年，沙田大會堂落成。

稍後，包括新翠邨、隆亨邨、秦石邨、美林邨及博康邨等多個公共屋邨先後落成，沙田新市鎮的發展也接近完成。

Introduction

The starting point of the tour is in Sha Tin.

Sha Tin was previously called "Lek Yuen" (literally means clear river in Chinese), and within the district there are Tai Wai, Fo Tan and Ma Liu Shui. Mountains like Beacon Hill, Lion Rock and Tate's Cairn are also situated in the district. In 1899, Sha Tin was put under Kowloon section while Ma On Shan, which is on the opposite side of Sha Tin Hoi, was put under Dong Hoi section, due to its proximity to the Sai Kung Peninsula.

In the early days, people from Sha Tin needed to climb over a mountain (the area around Shatin Pass Road nowadays) to go to Kowloon City, which was a hard journey. Not until 1902 after Tai Po Road was built that the villagers could go on foot or transport agricultural produce to districts like Sham Shui Po and Yau Ma Tei. In 1910, Kowloon-Canton Railway commenced service and the transportation between Kowloon and the New Territories was greatly improved.

In March 1911, the Hong Kong Aircraft Club performed test flights in Sha Tin Village (the area around Lek Yuen nowadays). They succeeded in taking off the plane to 60 feet high finally on 27 March after consecutive failures.

Until the 1950's, Sha Tin was still a farmland. After World War II, reclamation was carried out outside the railway station to build Sha Tin Hui. Half of the market was completed in 1950. In the same year, Grand Universal Salvation Rituals was held to commemorate the 60th anniversary of the renovation of Che Kung Temple.

In 1952, Sha Tin Hui was completed. There were a market and a pig-breeding cooperative. An agricultural products exhibition was also held in Sha Tin Hui in the same year. Later, a theatre and some restaurants were set up there. In those days, around 5,000 people from Hong Kong Island and Kowloon would travel to Sha Tin every week, to visit attractions like Amah Rock, Tao Fong Shan, Ten Thousand Buddhas Monastery and Sai Lam Temple. Tai Wai Railway Station was built in 1951.

At the same time, a lot of retired civil and military officials from the mainland would retreat as peasants on the mid-level of the mountain on top of Sha Tin Railway Station.

In November 1955, Sha Tin set up the altar

of the Da Jiu Festival, which was conducted once every ten years. The custom included inviting Che Kung to the altar, and the Tai Po district officer, dressed in traditional Chinese clothing, would inaugurate the light-on ceremony. A lot of people from the urban area would visit the ceremony.

In the same year, a new railway station was built in Ma Liu Shui to accommodate the relocation of the Chung Chi College from Caine Road. The railway station was renamed as University Station in 1969 when the Chinese University of Hong Kong moved in.

In 1958, Ma Liu Shui Ferry Pier was put in use. On 22 March, the world largest orphanage, Wu Kai Sha Children's Garden, opened in Ma On Shan. In the early 1970's, I often travelled to Tap Mun, Tung Ping Chau as well as Kat O by ferry from Ma Liu Shui.

In 1962, typhoon "Wanda" approached Hong Kong and Sha Tin was severely devastated, causing many casualties.

The two tubes of Lion Rock Tunnel from Kowloon to Sha Tin were opened in 1967 and 1978 respectively. It had greatly improved the transportation between the New Territories and the urban areas.

In 1969, the government decided to develop Sha Tin into a new town, in which several housing estates and a new racecourse would be built. The racecourse was opened on 7 Oct 1978.

Lek Yuen Estate, the first public housing estate derived from the farmland, was completed in 1976.

In 1985, Tolo Highway connecting Sha Tin and Sheung Shui was opened.

Sha Tin Town Hall was completed in 1986.

Later, a number of public housing estates including Sun Chui Estate, Lung Hang Estate, Chun Shek Estate, Mei Lam Estate, and Pok Hong Estate were completed one after the other. The development of Sha Tin new town was nearly completed.

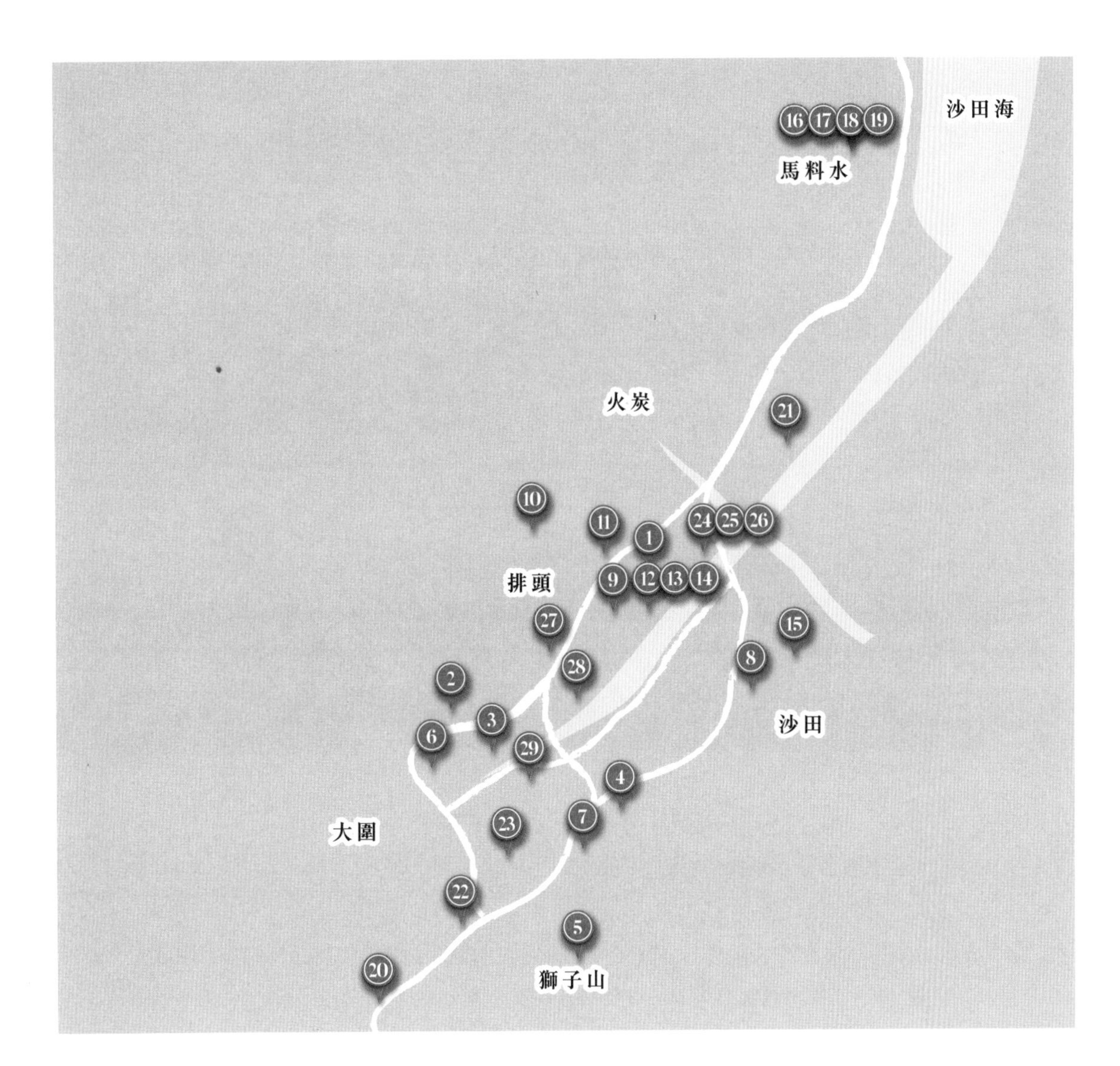

Please scan the below QR code for English map.

於 1911 年 3 月舉行的沙田飛機「試演」。

經過多次失敗後，飛機終在 3 月 27 日飛上 60 呎高空。起飛點約為現時沙田瀝源邨所在，背景為圓洲角。左中部的棚蓬是供港督盧吉專用，當時港督並不在場。

On 27 March 1911, a biplane taking off at Sha Tin from the plain, where Lek Yuen Estate is situated today. Yuen Chau Kok is at the background.

沙田大圍春耕的景象，約 1952 年。

Spring sowing at Tai Wai, Sha Tin, c. 1952.

沙田大圍，約 1970 年。

背景為沙田嶺。右方為城門河。左方為大埔公路。圖片正中現為美林邨。

Tai Wai, Sha Tin, c. 1970. Sha Tin Heights is at the background. Shing Mun River is on the right. Tai Po Road is on the left. The area at the centre is where Mei Lam Estate located today.

由沙田嶺一帶望向獅子山，1960 年代。

鐵路橋背後為紅梅谷。右方為顯徑及田心村一帶。

Lion Rock, looking from Sha Tin Heights, 1960's. At the back of the railway is Hung Mui Kuk. Hin Keng and Tin Sam Village are on the right.

沙田
大圍

由獅子山一帶俯瞰望夫石及沙田海，約 1965 年。

正中伸出海面的是馬料水，所在現為香港中文大學及馬場一帶。該處海域於 1970 年代起被填平，縮窄為現時的城門河。

Amah Rock and Sha Tin Harbour, looking from Lion Rock, c. 1965. The headland stretches out into the sea is the site of the Chinese University of Hong Kong and the racecourse nowadays. Most of Sha Tin Harbour was reclaimed in the 1970's. All that was left being the narrow channel of Shing Mun River.

攝於大圍火車站前的郊遊客，1955 年。

站於正中的是圖片提供者梁紹桔先生。

Travellers in front of Tai Wai Railway Station, 1955.

由獅子山隧道公路望向紅梅谷一帶，約 1974 年。

正中位於紅梅谷路的地盤，正在興建住宅屋苑世界花園。右上方為望夫石。

Hung Mui Kuk, looking from Lion Rock Tunnel Road, c.1974. The World-Wide Gardens which was under construction is at the centre. Amah Rock is on the upper right.

位於沙田頭的山下圍，亦稱「曾大屋」，約 1970 年。

「曾大屋」於 1867 年建成，為沙田最大的客家古屋，其隔鄰是博康邨。

Shan Ha Wai (Tsang Tai Uk), c. 1970. It is the biggest Hakka residence of Sha Tin Tau, completed in 1867. Pok Hong Estate is next to it.

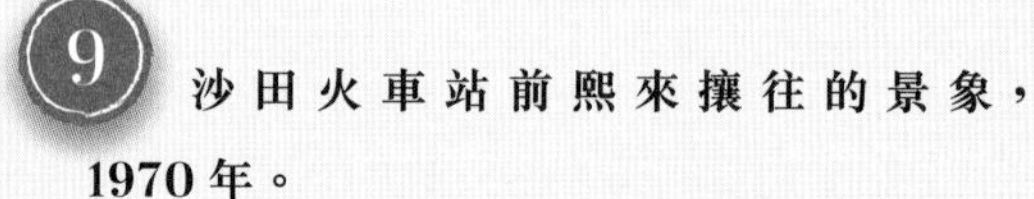

沙田火車站前熙來攘往的景象，1970年。

（圖片由梁紹桔先生提供）

People crowded the pavement in front of Sha Tin Railway Station, 1970.

10 沙田排頭坑旁、位於半山的萬佛寺及萬佛塔，約1965年。

當時為沙田規模最大的寺廟，內有一尊於1952年由利園山移至的觀音像。

The tower of Ten Thousand Buddhas Monastery, the biggest temple in Sha Tin, c. 1965. There is a status of Kun Yam in the temple which was relocated from Lee Garden Hill in 1952.

位於沙田火車站附近，一如遊樂場的西林寺，約 1952 年。

該處每逢假日遊人不絕如縷。圖為寺中園林間之放生亭。寺旁亦有多間食肆和多個食檔。

A pavilion in the garden of Sai Lam Temple, a tourist spot near Sha Tin Railway Station, c. 1952.

沙田火車站對面的沙田墟內之食街，約 1960 年。

可見若干間酒家及菜館。左方為著名的楓林小館。

Restaurants and eateries on the street of Sha Tin Hui, situated on the opposite side of Sha Tin Railway Station, c. 1960.

位於沙田墟內的沙田戲院，約 1960 年。

Sha Tin Theatre inside Sha Tin Hui, c. 1960.

1962 年 9 月 1 日，颶風「溫黛」襲港後沙田墟食街滿目瘡痍之景象。

左方為楓林小館。正中深色貨車背後是沙田戲院。

The “eatery street” in Sha Tin Hui, after the attack of Typhoon “Wanda” on 1 September 1962.

碇泊於沙田墟對開海面的沙田畫舫海鮮艇，約 1965 年。

沙田畫舫海鮮艇約於 1963 年開業。

The Sha Tin Floating Restaurant, in front of Sha Tin Hui, c. 1965.

正在興建的香港中文大學校舍，約 1965 年。

The campus of the Chinese University of Hong Kong under construction, c. 1965.

剛遷入沙田馬料水的香港中文大學校舍，1969 年。

The campus of the Chinese University of Hong Kong, just moved to Ma Liu Shui, Sha Tin, 1969.

沙田

大圍

(18) **香港中文大學崇基學院及前方的運動場，約 1970 年。**

位於山上的教學樓仍在興建中。

Chung Chi College and the sports ground at the front, the Chinese University of Hong Kong, c. 1970.

(19) **崇基學院，約 1970 年。**

右上方為禮拜堂，左上方為一列新建教學樓。

Chung Chi College, the Chinese University of Hong Kong, c. 1970. The chapel is on the upper right and the newly-constructed academic buildings are on the upper left.

(20) **獅子山隧道及其背後的獅子山，約 1970 年。**

Lion Rock Tunnel and Lion Rock at the back, c. 1970.

18 / 19 | 20

正進行填海工程的沙田，約 1973 年。

馬場後來在這一帶建成。

Reclamation of Sha Tin in progress, c. 1973. The racecourse was later built in the area.

由獅子山公路望向沙田頭及大圍一帶，約 1975 年。

可見大致平整完成的城門河，以及左中部的紅梅谷路。這一帶現時為秦石邨、新翠邨及田心村等屋邨所在。左方最高的山峰是針山。

The area of Sha Tin Tau and Tai Wai, looking from Lion Rock Tunnel Road, c. 1975. Shing Mun River which is almost completed can be seen in the picture. Hung Mui Kuk Road, where Chun Shek Estate, Sun Tsui Estate and Tin Sam Village are situated today, is on the middle left. Cham Shan (Needle Hill) is on the left.

23 約 1975 年的沙田。

前中部可見獅子山隧道收費站。正中的高樓為興建中的住宅屋苑世界花園。左方為大圍區。城門河旁可見興建中、位於圓洲角兩端的沙角邨，其對面是瀝源邨及禾輋邨，以及位於半山的居者有其屋（居屋）穗禾苑。

Sha Tin, c. 1975. The toll station of Lion Rock Tunnel is at the middle front. The tall building at the centre is World-Wide Gardens. Various public housing estates are being constructed on the banks of Shing Mun River.

約 1977 年的城門河兩岸。

正中可見已落成入伙的瀝源邨及禾輋邨。馬場工程也大致完成，於 1978 年落成啟用。城門河右端正在闢建大涌橋路，其旁邊的圓洲角一帶正在興建若干座公共屋邨及私人屋苑富豪花園等。

Shing Mun River, c. 1977. Lek Yuen Estate and Wo Che Estate are at the centre. The racecourse is almost completed and was later opened in 1978. Tai Chung Kiu Road, which is under construction, is on the right.

沙田城門河，約 1976 年。

左方可見已落成的瀝源邨。其前方可見沙田畫舫。右方是興建中的禾輋邨。左下方為圓洲角一帶。

Shing Mun River, c. 1976. Lek Yuen Estate is on the left and Wo Che Estate is on the right. The Sha Tin Floating Restaurant is in front of Lek Yuen Estate.

沙田
大圍

26 由圓洲角望向剛落成的瀝源邨及前方的沙田畫舫，約 1975 年。

Lek Yuen Estate, looking from Yuen Chau Kok, c. 1975. The Sha Tin Floating Restaurant is on the upper right.

一列火車正駛近沙田站，約 1955 年。

圖中背景為馬鞍山。當時的海邊仍是一片寧靜。

A train approaching Sha Tin Station, c. 1955. Ma On Shan is at the background.

28 1980 年代後期，正在參觀沙田新市鎮的姬鵬飛先生。

Mr. Ji Pengfei visited the Sha Tin New Town in the late 1980's.

29 位於沙田大圍新田村、於 1914 年建成的慈航淨苑，約 1948 年。

（圖片由巫羽階先生提供）

Chi Hong Ching Yuen in San Tin Village, Tai Wai, Sha Tin, c. 1948.

路線五

大埔探索遊

Route 5

Discovery Tour on Tai Po

前言

大埔，早期名為「大步」，其對開之大埔海（吐露港）以盛產珍珠馳名，已有過千年歷史。

十七世紀後期，大埔及太和建立規模龐大的墟市，當時與上水石湖墟及元朗墟齊名。

1899 年，英國從大埔開始接管新界，隨即在該處設立新界的行政中心，當時大埔隸屬於雙魚全約。

1902 年，連接深圳及九龍市區的大埔道（公路）落成，加上稍後築成、連接上水及元朗的公路，以及 1910 年通車的九廣鐵路，使大埔旋即成為新界主要區域。同時，大埔墟（舊墟）的重要性已被火車站旁的太和墟所取代。二、三十年代，富善街以及木製之廣福橋一帶，為大埔最繁盛之地區。淪陷時期，因交通不便，大埔陷於停頓，和平後才恢復發展。

1952 年，大埔林村至元朗錦田的林錦公路通車。同時，嘉道理家族在公路旁設立畜牧模範場，扶助農民推廣農牧生產，此為嘉道理農場前身。該家族又於 1956 年在大埔創辦一間太平地氈廠。

1954 年，大埔林村舉行十年一度的太平清醮，蓋設多座醮棚及一個可容納數千人之大戲棚，以供村民「睇大戲」（觀賞粵劇）。

1955 年，大埔範圍內的沙頭角公路改名為汀角路。

1956 年 2 月，新界民政署長彭德（Kenneth Myer Arthur Barnett）在大埔元洲仔官邸舉行園遊會，設筵百席招待新界商紳。

繼荃灣之後，當局於 1960 年計劃將大埔發展為一個現代化商住之衛星城市。1972 年，政府推行大埔的大型發展計劃。

大埔元洲仔為漁民聚居地，有大量艇屋，衛生條件惡劣，生活環境甚差。至 1976 年，當局在元洲仔進行填海，在此興建公共屋邨廣福邨。同時，亦在船灣進行填海，以興建香港第一座工業邨——大埔工業邨。

1980 年代中，大埔新市鎮已為過百萬人提供居所。

1990 年代初，由大埔連接各區的新道路包括吐露港公路等完成後，大埔對外的交通進一步完善。

Introduction

Tai Po was previously called "big step" (in Chinese). Tolo Harbour outside Tai Po abounded in pearls and already had more than a thousand year of history.

In the late seventeen century, huge markets were established in Tai Po and Tai Wo, comparable to those in Sheung Shui and Yuen Long.

The British took over the New Territories, starting from Tai Po, in 1899. The administration centre of the New Territories was then set up in Tai Po, which was put under Sheung Yue section.

In 1902, Tai Po Road connecting Shenzhen and Kowloon was completed. Tai Po Road, together with the road connecting Sheung Shui and Yuen Long, and Kowloon-Canton Railway which opened in 1910, had converted Tai Po into a major district in the New Territories. At the same time, Tai Po Hui was gradually replaced by Tai Wo Hui next to the railway station. In the 1920's and 1930's, the areas around Fu Shin Street and the wooden Kwong Fuk Bridge were the most flourished districts in Tai Po. However, Tai Po was brought to a stand due to insufficient transportation during Japanese occupation, and only resumed its development after World War II.

In 1952, Lam Kam Road connecting Lam Tsuen in Tai Po and Kam Tin in Yuen Long opened. The Kardoorie family set up husbandry model plant next to the road at the same time. The plant helped promote agricultural production in the village and was later transformed into Kardoorie Farm. Tai Ping Carpets factory was also established by the Kardoorie family in Tai Po in 1956.

In 1954, the Da Jiu Festival, held once every ten years, was held in Lam Tsuen, Tai Po. A number of altars and a large theatre for showing Cantonese opera, with a capacity of several thousand people, were set up.

The section of Sha Tau Kok Road within the Tai Po district was renamed as Ting Kok Road in 1955.

In February 1956, Kenneth Barnett, the Secretary for Home Affairs, held a fun fair in his official residence in Yuen Chau Tsai, Tai Po. More than 1,000 squires and businessman attended the fair.

In 1960, the authority planned to develop Tai Po into a modernized commercial and residential satellite city after Tsuen Wan. The government later implemented the large-scale Tai Po development project in 1972.

Yuen Chau Tsai in Tai Po was previously a settlement of fishermen. They lived in boathouses where living condition was unsatisfactory with bad hygiene. In 1976, the authority carried out reclamation in Yuen Chau Tsai and Kwong Fuk Estate was later built on the reclaimed land. Land was also obtained from reclamation in Plover Cove to establish Tai Po Industrial Estate, the first industrial estate in Hong Kong.

In the mid 1980's, the Tai Po new town had provided residence to over one million people.

In the early 1990's, new roads connecting Tai Po with other districts, including Tolo Highway, were completed. The transportation to and from Tai Po was greatly improved.

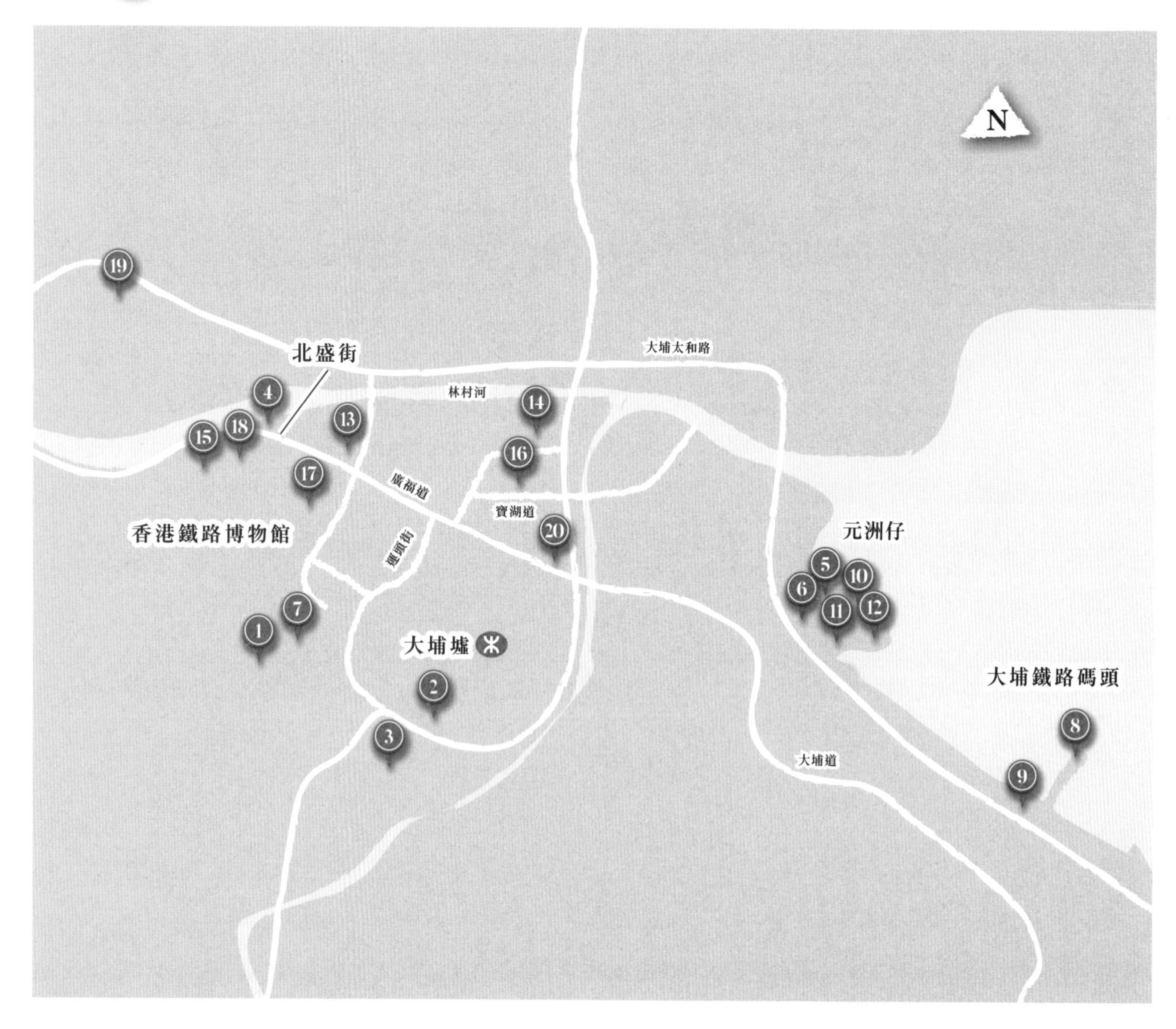

Please scan the below QR code for English map.

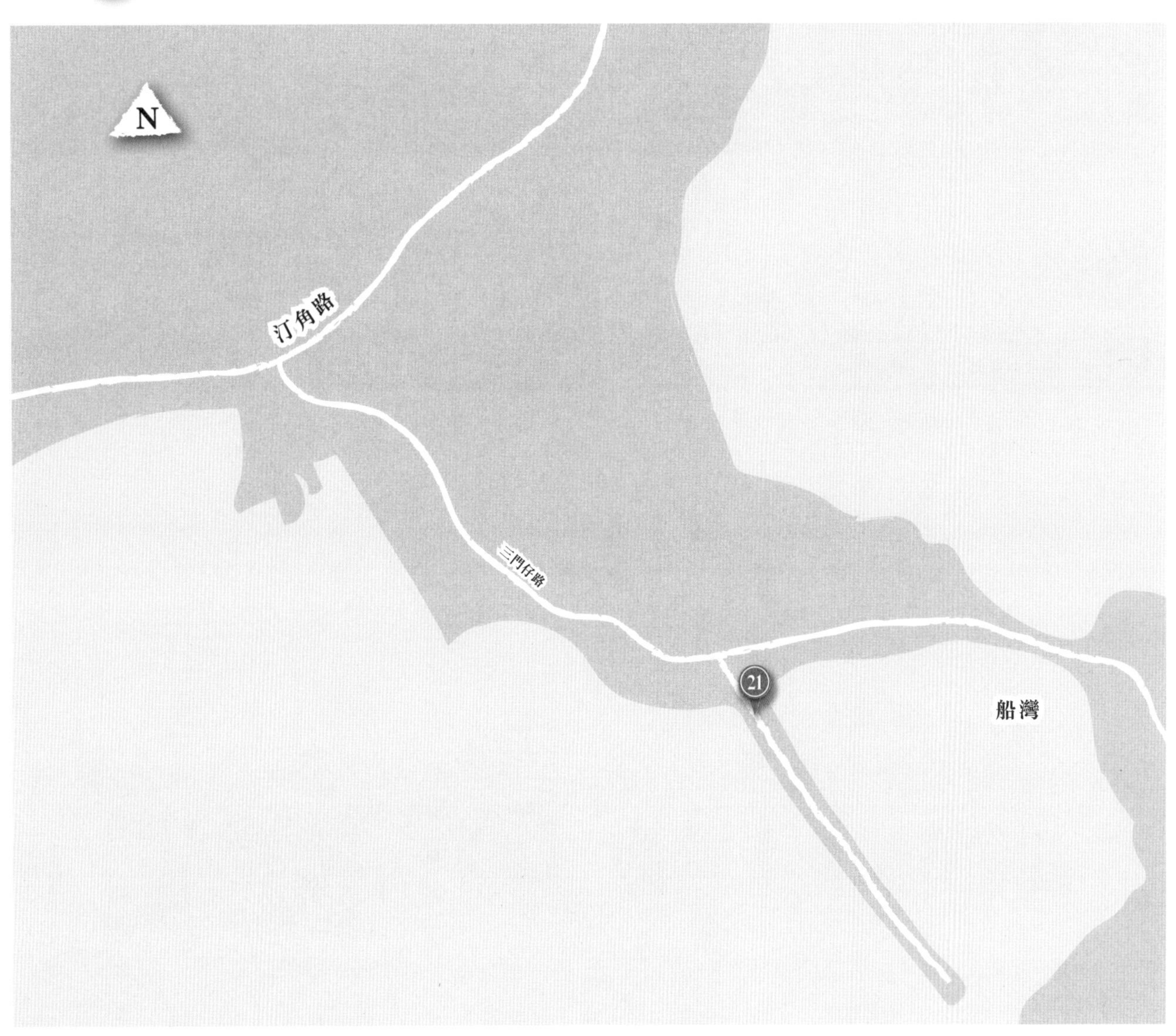

Please scan the below QR code for English map.

沙田

大圍

1899年4月16日，英軍在大埔舉行接收新界儀式。

圖中可見一個為儀式而蓋搭的草棚。當時大埔村民與英方軍警對峙。接收儀式由輔政司駱克及警察總監梅軒利主持。稍後村民隨即作出反抗，但遭英軍鎮壓。

The ceremony of the takeover of the New Territories, held at Tai Po on 16 April 1899 by the Colonial Secretary, Sir James Haldane Stewart Lockhart and the Superintendent of the Police, Sir Francis Henry May. Villagers rioted against the takeover but was suppressed.

位於大埔河畔大埔墟火車站旁、落成於1907年的裁判署及田土廳，約1920年。

（圖片由香港歷史博物館提供）

Tai Po Magistracy and Land Registry, completed in 1907, beside Tai Po River, c. 1920.

1899年在大埔運頭塘山上興建的大埔警署。

警署於1900年全部落成，圖為當時的情景。

Tai Po Police Station on Wan Tau Tong Shan, Tai Po, completed in 1900.

1 | 2
3

PAK SHING STREET
北盛街

沙田

大圍

1941年12月8日，日軍入侵新界及九龍，軍隊途經大埔北盛街。

On 8 December 1941, the Japanese troops invaded Kowloon and the New Territories, passing through Pak Shing Street, Tai Po.

經過大埔元洲仔一帶的九廣火車，約 1950 年。

圖片正中為吐露港。

A Kowloon Canton Railway train passing through Yuen Chau Tsai, Tai Po, c. 1950. Tolo Harbour is at the centre.

從錦山一帶望向大埔，約 1951 年。

圖右方是大埔墟。正中是元洲仔。

Tai Po, looking from Kam Shan, c. 1951. Yuen Chau Tsai is in the middle and Tai Po Hui is on the right.

大埔墟，約 1955 年。

圖中可見一間炳記茶室，兩名漁民在其前方曝曬鹹魚。

Two fishermen drying salty fish in front of a teahouse in Tai Po Hui, c. 1955.

5 | 6 | 7

大埔滘，約 1960 年。

正中為大埔滘碼頭。左方為元洲仔。

Tai Po Kau, c. 1960. Tai Po Kau Pier is in the middle. Yuen Chau Tsai is on the left.

大埔滘火車站，1981 年。

這個於 1910 年落成的火車站，早期名為大埔站，約 1965 年改名為大埔滘站，自 1983 年 5 月起停用。(圖片由何其鋭先生提供)

Tai Po Kau Railway Station, 1981. The station was completed in 1910 and was formerly called Tai Po Railway Station. Its name was changed to Tai Po Kau Railway Station in 1965 and later cancelled from May 1983.

沙田
大圍

從元洲仔一帶望向左方的八仙嶺，約 1965 年。

Pat Sin Leng, looking from Yuen Chau Tsai, c. 1965.

大埔元洲仔艇屋區，約 1962 年。

大量水上人居於這些由破舊船艇改成的水上寮屋，稱為「住家艇」。當中亦有商店、學校、食肆以至教堂。艇民生活條件惡劣，遭到社會嚴厲批評，後來當局於 1970 年代後期興建大量公共屋邨以作安置。

Floating homes (boats) which never set to sea, jammed at Yuen Chau Tsai, Tai Po, c. 1962. There were also floating shops, schools, restaurants as well as a church. The living condition of the floating population was extremely poor. Most of the people moved to public housing estates in the late 1970's.

約 1965 年農曆新年期間，元洲仔艇戶的景象。

Floating homes at Yuen Chau Tsai, during the Lunar New Year, c. 1965.

10
11 | 12

大埔廣福道，約 1960 年。

這一帶當年是郊遊客的中心點。金都戲院旁是安富道。

Kwong Fuk Road, a tourist centre in Tai Po, c. 1960. On Fu Road is besides Kam To Cinema (the second building on the left).

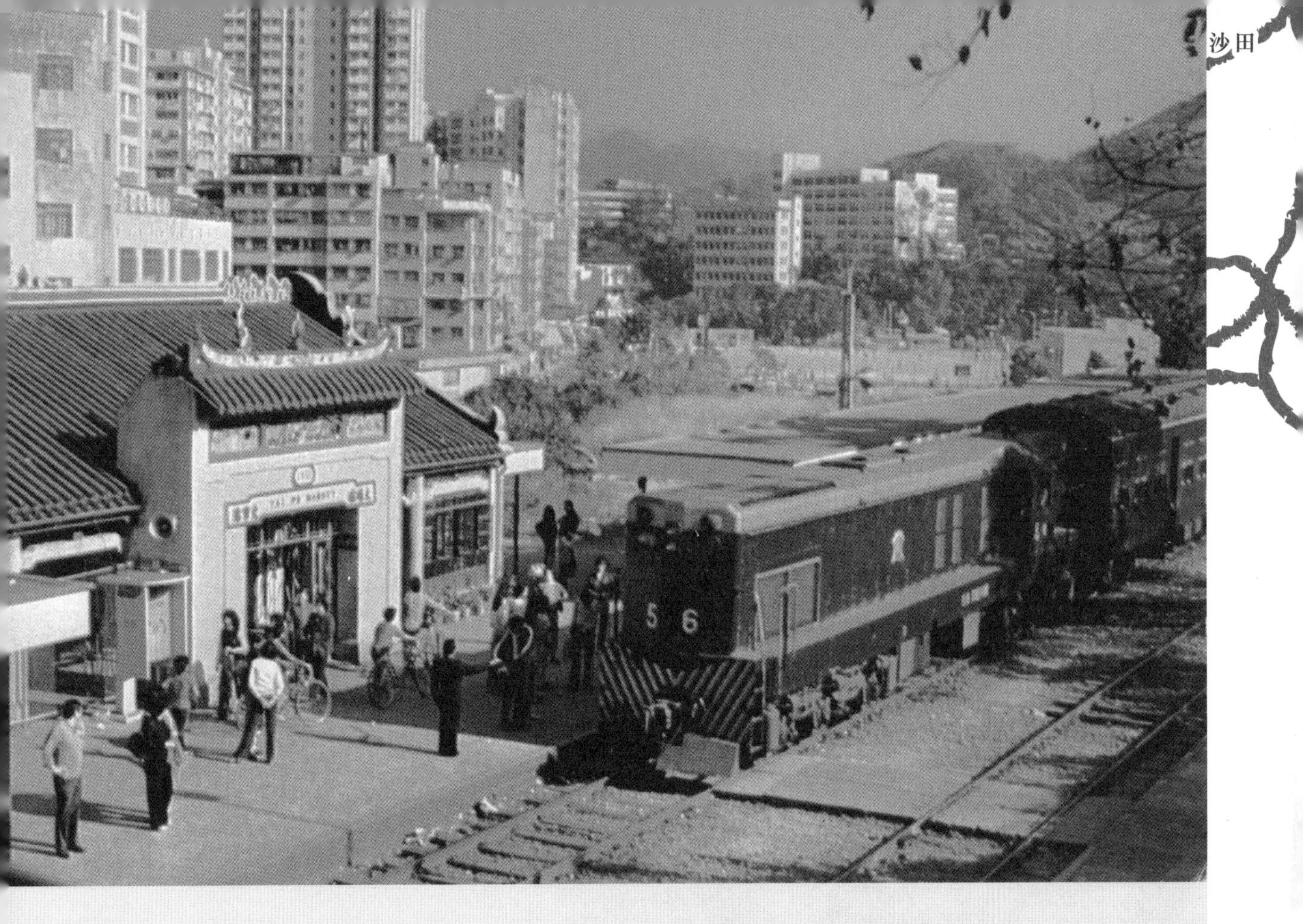

於 1913 年落成的舊大埔墟火車站，約 1980 年。

圖中可見一列柴油發動的火車。該火車站於 1985 年變身為香港鐵路博物館。

The old Tai Po Market Railway Station, completed in 1913, c. 1980. A diesel train is at the station. The station was fully restored and became the Hong Kong Railway Museum in 1985.

一座位於大埔的龍船廠棚，約 1960 年。

大埔賽龍為每年端午節一大盛事。

A dragon boat shipyard in Tai Po, c. 1960. Dragon boat racing is famous in Tai Po in the earlier days.

大埔寶湖道上的會景巡遊，1970年。

左方由填海獲致的地段稍後建成住宅寶湖花園。

Traditional festival dragon dance on Plover Cove Road, Tai Po, c. 1970. The reclaimed open space on the left is where the Plover Cove Garden situated today.

大埔鄉事委員會辦事處，1981年。

其前身為於1892年成立的大埔七約鄉公所。（圖片由何其鋭先生提供）

The Tsat Yeuk Rural Committee established in 1892, Tai Po, 1981.

位於大埔北盛街一帶的攤檔，1981年。

右方為林村河。(圖片由何其鋭先生提供)

Stalls in the market area on Pak Shing Street, Tai Po, 1981. Lam Tsuen River is on the right.

位於大埔雲山山腳的松園仙館，內有遊樂場和酒家，約 1965 年。

Greenville Amusement Park with restaurant, at the foot of Wan Shan, Tai Po, c. 1965.

20 由大埔河望向廣福道，約 1953 年。

（圖片由巫羽階先生提供）

Kwong Fuk Road, looking from Tai Po River, c. 1953.

21 大埔大美（尾）督船灣淡水湖的主壩，約 1968 年。

The main dam of Plover Cove Reservoir, Tai Mei Tuk, Tai Po, c. 1968.

路線六

新界北區發展遊（粉嶺、上水、沙頭角及羅湖）

Route 6

Tour on the Development of the North District (Fanling, Sheung Shui, Sha Tau Kok and Lo Wu)

前言

1899年，上水及粉嶺被劃入雙魚全約。而沙頭角則為一獨立全約，屬下有禾坑、鹿頸、谷埔及蓮麻坑等分約。1900年，雙魚及沙頭角分別編入新訂之第八約和第十約。

粉嶺、上水、沙頭角及打鼓嶺等地區，因位於新界東北部，與深圳相連，被名為「北區」。北區亦包括吉澳及塔門等島嶼。1909年，曾發生一宗位於大鵬灣（馬士灣）吉澳島海面的擄人勒索案。

1932年，上水石湖墟舉行農產品展覽會。1938年的一屆改在粉嶺舉行，由港督羅富國（Sir Geoffrey Alexander Stafford Northcote）剪綵。

1930年代，北區對外的主要幹道，有由粉嶺至凹頭的青山道（公路），瀕臨深圳河及后海灣的下游，其中有一條名為落馬洲大道（落馬洲站）的支路。此外，亦有粉嶺至沙頭角的沙頭角公路，以及沙頭角經打鼓嶺至上水的大道。

1948年3月8日，新界粉嶺聯和公司闢建聯和墟墟市，招承舖位，墟市於1949年11月落成。

當時的另一大墟市為上水之石湖墟，內有兩座新落成的魚市場。上水亦是穀米的集中地。當局後來又在石湖墟籌建新街市。

1949年6月起，上水、沙頭角、打鼓嶺及落馬洲等地，由晚上10時至凌晨6時實施戒嚴，有事外出者須領特別通行證。直到1953年，新界多處包括粉嶺等區仍實施戒嚴。同時，亦包括成為特別禁區的沙頭角中英街。

1950年，古洞及粉嶺安樂村等區設立了若干個農民合作社，以便管理及集運農產品，和發展農民福利事業。

同年7月，由粉嶺至錦田的粉錦公路通車。

1954年6月19日，上水石湖戲院開幕。

1955年2月21日，石湖墟全墟被焚毀，災民5,000人，為新界史上最大的火災。在災區重建的新商戶市場，於同年7月18日由新界民政署長彭德主持開幕，而石湖墟亦着手重建。可是，1956年12月23日，石湖墟發生第二次大火，重建工程要到1964年3月才告完成。村民在新墟市重建後舉行會景巡遊慶祝。

1956年4月4日，上水消防局啟用，備有兩部告魯式消防車服務各鄉村。同年，石湖墟、聯和墟，以至大埔及沙田等墟市，亦紛紛安裝螢光路燈以照明。

同年 7 月，洪水沖毀邊境近十英里的鐵絲網，以致門禁大開，偷渡者活躍，警方於上水實施宵禁。

1957 年，由上水連接粉嶺及大埔的交通要道馬會道築成。

1958 年 9 月，塔門的新碼頭啟用。另一離島吉澳，有一作為養珠場的海段，於 1972 年改作魚排。1970 年代初，筆者不時在這一帶連同包括東平洲及吉澳的離島遊覽及暢泳。現在回想起來其實危機四伏，因為多個離島的魚檔均可見大量一尺多長的鯊魚仔出售，可見這裏有不少鯊魚出沒。

Introduction

Since 1899, Sheung Shui and Fanling were put under Sheung Yue section. Sha Tau Kok was a section on its own, under which there were subsections including Wo Hang, Luk Keng, Kuk Po and Lin Ma Hang. In 1900, Sheung Yue section and Sha Tau Kok section were rearranged into new section eight and section ten respectively.

Districts including Fanling, Sheung Shui, Sha Tau Kok and Ta Kwu Ling are situated at the northeastern side of the New Territories, connecting Shenzhen. They are collectively known as North District. Outlying islands like Kat O and Tap Mun are also within North District. In 1909, a case of kidnapping for ransom happened near Kat O at Mirs Bay.

An agricultural products exhibition was held in Shek Wu Hui in Sheung Shui in 1932. In 1938, the exhibition was moved to Fanling, with Governor Northcote hosting the ribbon-cutting ceremony.

In the 1930's, one of the major routes to and from North District was Castle Peak Road, which travelled from Fanling to Au Tau. There was a branch road, called Lok Ma Chau Main Road, which was close to Shenzhen River and the lower course of Hau Hoi Wan (Deep Bay). Other routes included Sha Tau Kok Road, which travelled from Fanling to Sha Tau Kok, and another one which travelled from Sha Tau Kok, via Ta Kwu Ling to Sheung Shui.

On 8 March 1948, Luen Wo Company in Fanling developed Luen Wo Hui and pre-sold the units. The market was completed in November 1949.

At the same time, Shek Wu Hui in Sheung Shui was another large market, within which were two newly-built seafood markets. All grains and rice mustered in Sheung Shui. Later, a new market was established in Shek Wu Hui.

Since June 1949, martial law was enforced from 10pm to 6am in districts like Sheung Shui, Sha Tau Kok, Ta Kwu Ling and Lok Ma Chau. Special permit was needed for going out within the time period. Until 1953, martial law was still enforced in several districts in the New Territories, including Fanling. Chung Ying Street in Sha Tau Kok became a special closed area at the same time.

In 1950, agricultural cooperatives were set up in districts like Kwu Tung and On Lok Tsuen in Fanling. The aims were to better manage and consolidate agricultural produce, as well as to promote the welfare of the peasants.

In July 1950, Fan Kam Road, which travelled from Fanling to Kam Tin, opened.

On 19 June 1954, Shek Wu Theatre opened in Sheung Shui.

On 21 February 1955, a fire broke out in Shek Wu Hui and the market was completely destroyed, causing 5,000 victims. It was the most serious fire in the history of the New Territories. New shops were established in the disaster area later and Kenneth Barnett, the Secretary of Home Affairs, was the guest of the opening ceremony held on 18 July 1955. Shek Wu Hui was under reconstruction at the same time. On 23 December 1956, however, another fire broke out in Shek Wu Hui, resulting in an extension of the reconstruction until March 1964. Celebrative parade was held by villagers after the new market was completed.

On 4 April 1956, a fire station, equipped with two fire engines to provide services to villages, opened in Sheung Shui. In the same year, fluorescent street lamps were installed in Shek Wu Hui, Luen Wo Hui and markets in Tai Po and Sha Tin.

In July 1956, the ten-mile wire fence at the border was destroyed by flood, resulting in a loophole in access control. To prevent illegal immigrants from sneaking in, curfew was imposed in Sheung Shui by the police.

In 1957, Jockey Club Road, a major route connecting Sheung Shui, Fanling and Tai Po was completed.

In September 1958, a new pier opened in Tap Mun. A part of the sea used as pearl farm previously at Kat O was converted into fish rafts in 1972. In the early 1970's, I often travelled and swam in the above-mentioned areas, as well as other outlying islands like Tung Ping Chau and Kat O. It seems threatening now when I recalled the experience as a large number of small sharks of one foot long were sold in fish stalls on those outlying islands. That means sharks were often present in those areas.

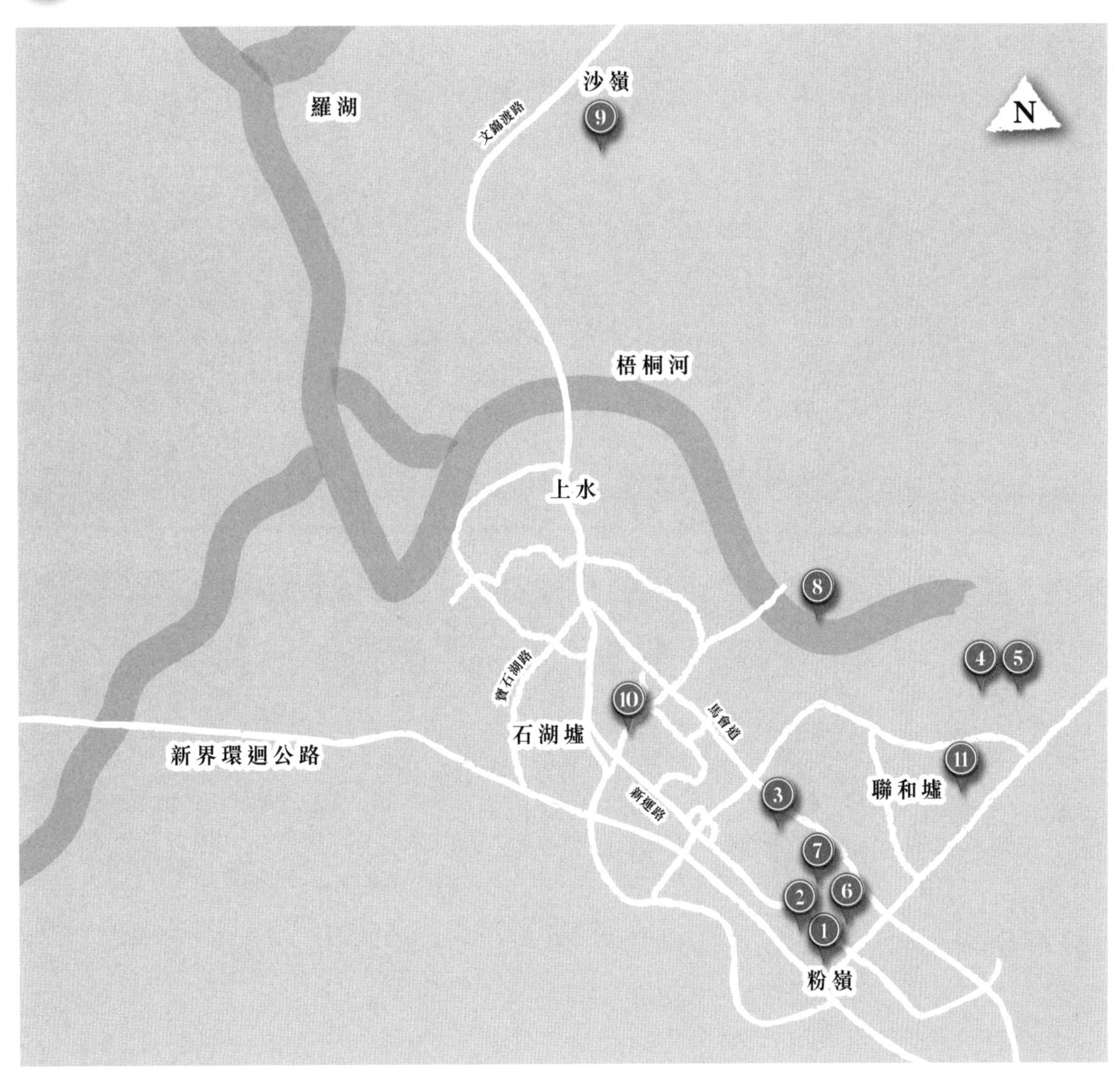

Please scan the below QR code for English map.

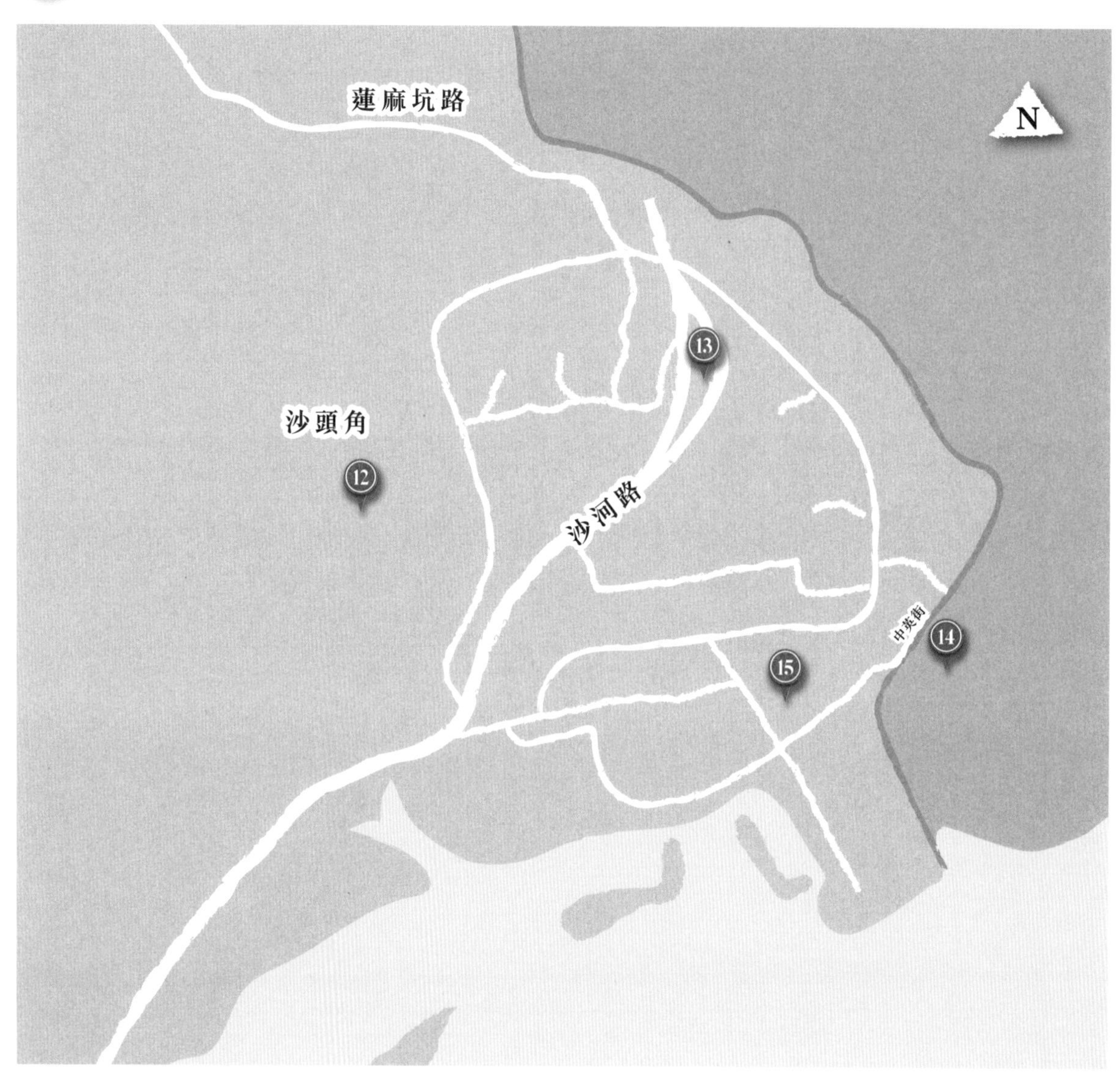

Please scan the below QR code for English map.

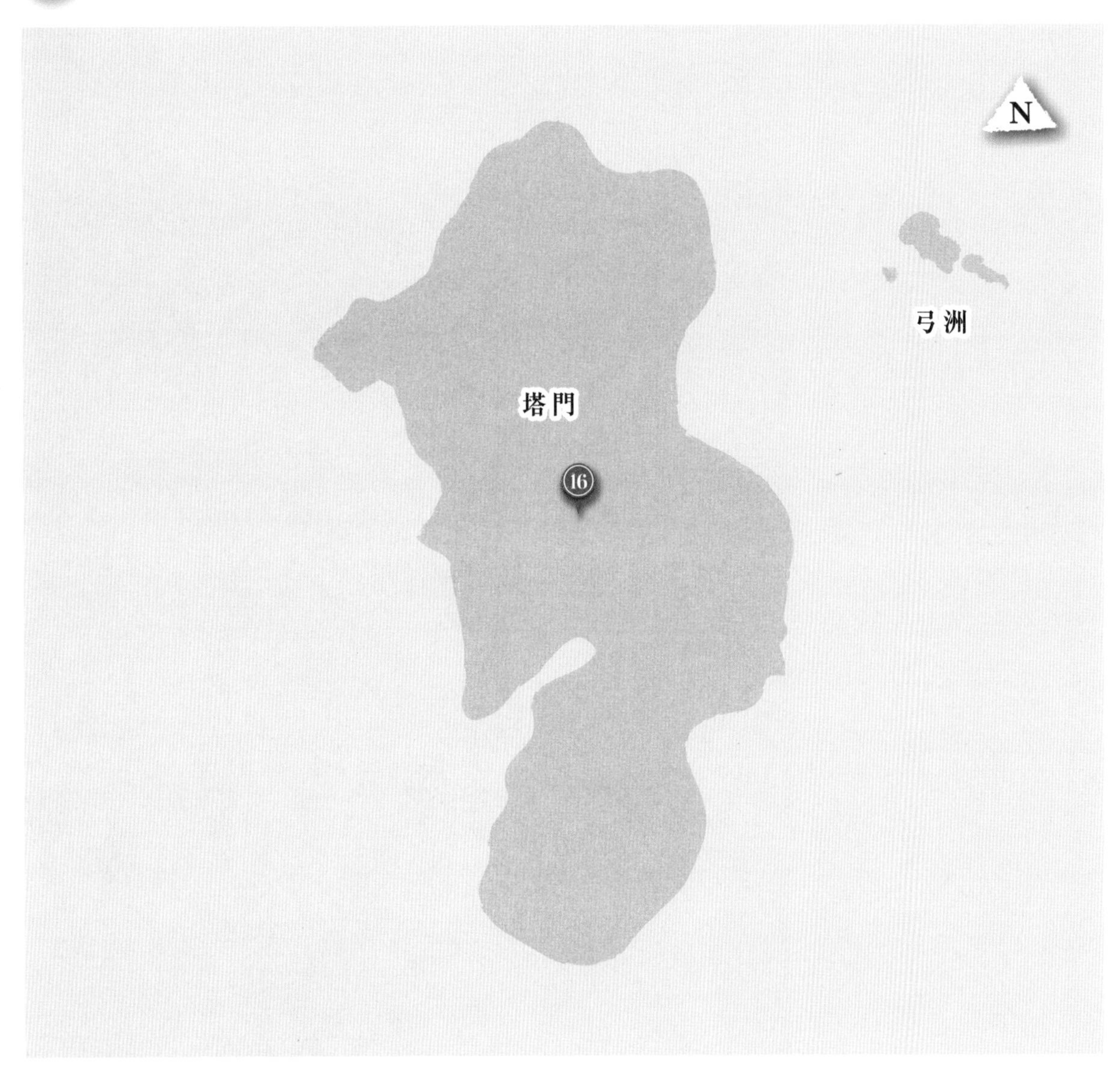

Please scan the below QR code for English map.

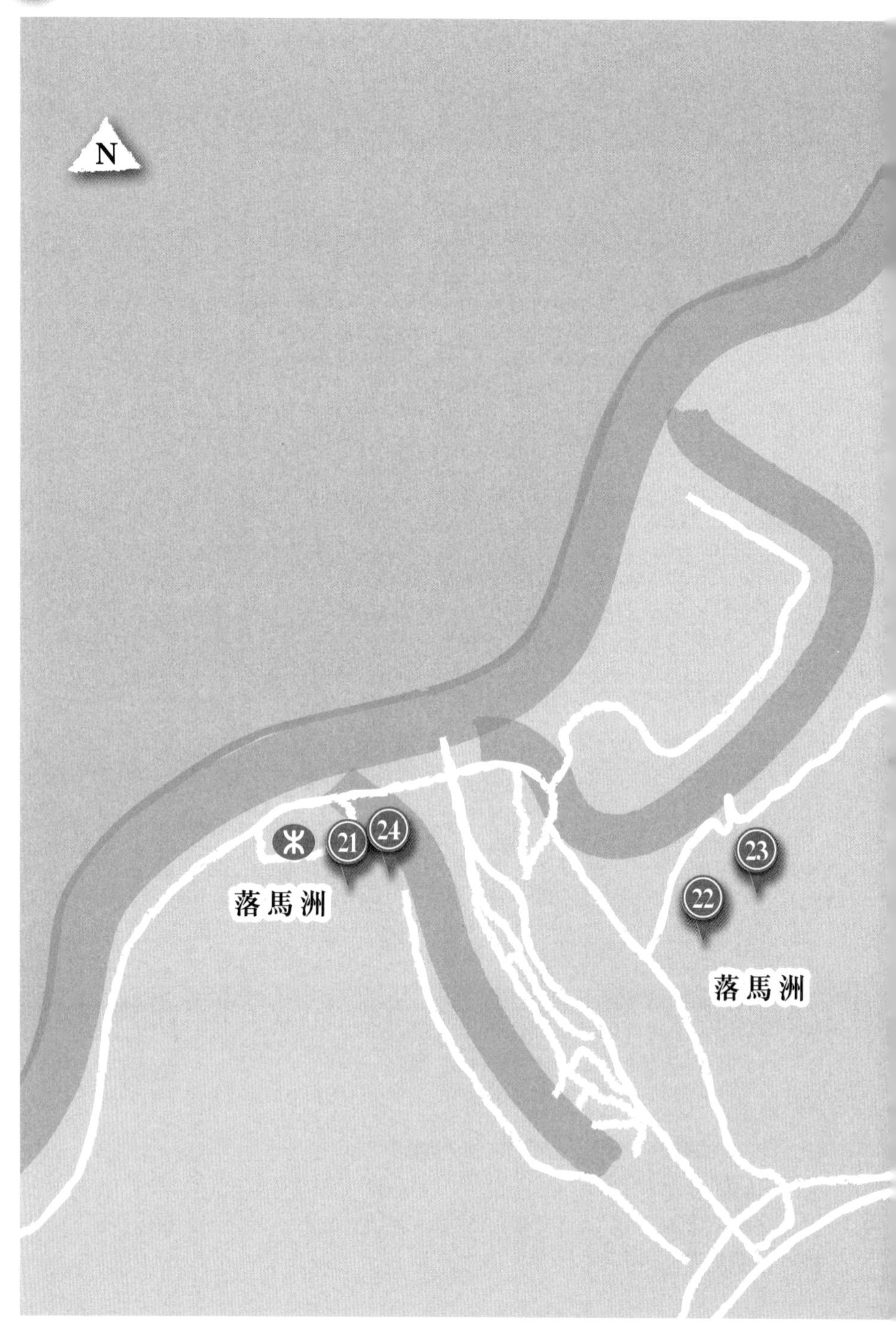

Please scan the below QR code for English map.

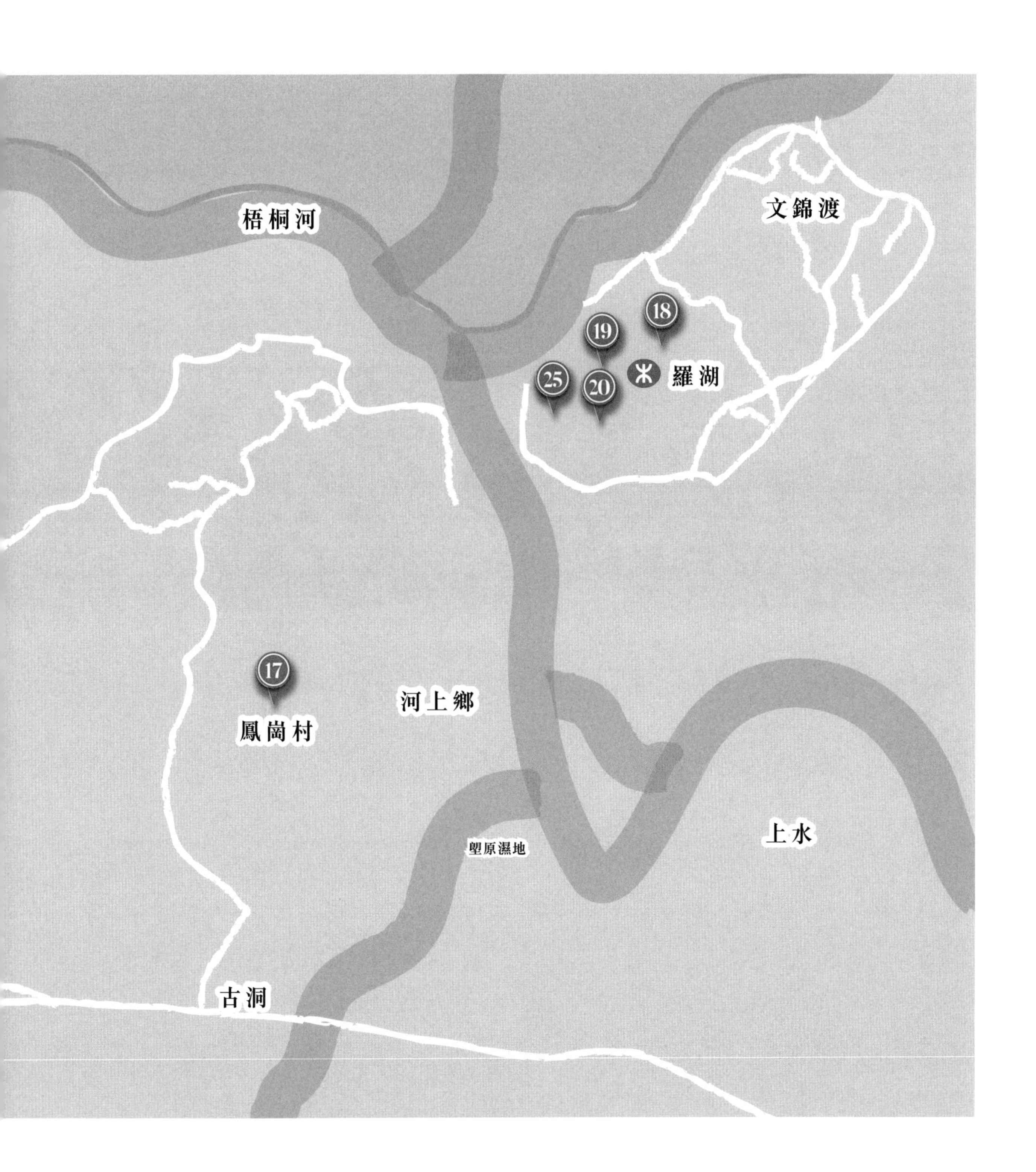
梧桐河
文錦渡
18
19
羅湖
25
20
17
河上鄉
鳳崗村
塱原濕地
上水
古洞

約 1915 年的粉嶺鐵路站。

所在現時為粉嶺公路及新運路一帶。（圖片由香港歷史博物館提供）

Fanling Railway Station, c. 1915. The location is now the area near San Wan Road and Fanling Highway.

一列停泊於粉嶺站的火車，約 1915 年。

A train at Fanling Railway Station, c. 1915.

粉嶺稻田上的春耕，1930 年代。

Spring sowing, Fanling, 1930's.

粉嶺新圍軍營，約 1933 年。

軍營前方為沙頭角公路。

The Gallipoli Lines on Sha Tau Kok Road, c. 1933.

新圍軍營近景，約 1930 年。

A closer shot of the Gallipoli Lines, c. 1930.

59
FANLING

適雅大酒家
RESTAURANT
BET

沙田

大圍

粉嶺火車站及一列柴油火車，1981 年。

（圖片由何其鋭先生提供）

A diesel train at Fanling Railway Station, 1981.

位於粉嶺火車站前的馬路上的若干食肆，1981 年。

（圖片由何其鋭先生提供）

Eateries on the road in front of Fanling Railway Station, 1981.

粉嶺梧桐河邊的村屋及水上棚屋，約 1965 年。

Village and stilt houses along the bank of Ng Tung River, Fanling, c. 1965.

6 | 7
8

位於邊境的沙嶺，約 1935 年。

圖中右方為深圳河。

Sha Ling in the border area, c. 1935.

Shenzhen (Sham Chun) River is on the right.

上水墟市石湖墟，約 1950 年。

Shek Wu Hui, Sheung Shui, c. 1950.

粉嶺聯和墟的聯和市場及魚市場，約 1950 年

圖中左方可見一間僑安大旅店。（圖片由巫羽階先生提供）

Luen Wo Market and the fish market in Luen Wo Hui, Fanling, c. 1950.

⑫ 沙頭角邊境區的秋收景象，約1910年。

Autumn harvest in Sha Tau Kok border area, c. 1910.

⑬ 沙頭角禁區的出入口管制站，約1919年。

The checkpoint in Sha Tau Kok closed area, c. 1919.

約 1982 年的沙頭角。

正中為中英街。前方為香港新界區，後方為內地區域。可見「深圳沙頭角進出口貿易公司」以及「綜合公司糖煙」的招牌。當年，因內地推行改革開放，在這裏進行的香港與內地商貿十分活躍。

Sha Tau Kok, c. 1982. Chung Ying (Sino-British) Street is at the centre. The place became prosperous from 1979 due to China's Open Door Policy.

沙頭角禁區，約 1982 年。

可見沙頭角海海旁的水上寮屋。沙頭角碼頭位於圖中左方。沙頭角海早期的英文名稱為 Starling Inlet，源於一艘名為 *Staling* 的英國軍艦。

The stilt houses along Sha Tau Kok Hoi (Starling Inlet) in the closed area, c. 1982.

塔門島上的村屋及居民，約 1960 年。

塔門島於 1899 年曾屬東島洞全約及沙頭角轄下。筆者曾於 1971 年在此目睹若干座用火水煤油燈作動力的電冰箱。在海旁可見大量小型鮑魚。令人印象深刻的景點包括相疊的「呂字石」。

Villagers and houses on Tap Mun, c. 1960. In 1899, Tap Mun had been an island under Tung Dou Tung section and Sha Tau Kok.

由鳳崗村（近古洞東方區）一帶望向河上鄉附近的羅湖軍營，1919 年。

圖中中後方為塱原濕地。

Lo Wu military camps, near Ho Sheung Heung, looking from Fung Kong Tsuen, 1919. Long Valley is at the middle back.

沙田
大圍

位於中英邊境的深圳河，約 1970 年。

羅湖橋兩端懸掛着中英國旗。深圳區當時仍是一大片禾田。

Sino-British border checkpoints on Lo Wu Bridge, over Shenzhen (Sham Chun) River, c. 1970.

經過羅湖橋的回鄉客，約 1975 年。

Train passengers crossing Lo Wu Bridge heading to mainland China, c.1975.

正駛過羅湖橋的省港直通列車，1979 年。

A through train from Guangzhou to Hong Kong, passing through Lo Wu Bridge, 1979.

21 **落馬洲邊境禁區的村民與外籍遊客，約 1964 年。**

在他們旁邊有一輛名為「紅牌車」的出租汽車。

Tourists and villagers at Lok Ma Chau closed area checkpoint, c. 1964.

22 **落馬洲瞭望亭及一帶的中外遊客，約 1970 年。**

Tourists and the sight-seeing pavilion at Lok Ma Chau, c. 1970 。

23 **忽略從落馬洲眺望深圳河及深圳區景色，約 1965 年。**

滿目盡是一大片一望無際的田野。

Shenzhen (Sham Chun) River and farmland, looking from Lok Ma Chau, c. 1965.

21/22 | 23

由落馬洲望向皇崗口岸一帶，約1990年。

圖右中部可見剛落成的聯檢大樓。

The Boundary Control Point at Huanggang in the border area, looking from Lok Ma Chau, c. 1990.

沙田

大圍

位於中英邊境羅湖橋的出入境管制站，約 1970 年。

Immigration Control Point at Lo Wu border, c. 1970.

路線七

元朗及屯門發展之旅

Route 7

Tour on the Development of Yuen Long and Tuen Mun

前言

元朗

1899年4月16日，英軍在大埔進行接收新界的儀式，由輔政司駱克（Sir James Haldane Stewart Lockhart）以及警察總監梅軒利（Sir Francis Henry May）負責（位於港島區的駱克道及梅道是以他們命名）。兩天後，英軍強攻元朗錦田的吉慶圍，隨後陸續進駐元朗、屯門以及其他新界地區。

同年，當局設立元朗全約，其附屬分約的村落計有十八鄉、錦田、平（屏）山、廈村、屯門及大欖涌等。

1900年，大部分元朗區被併入新訂之第六約，亦包括新田、天水圍及流浮山等區。

元朗墟（舊墟）於1670年成立，與大埔墟及石湖墟皆為新界主要墟市。1915年，位於合財街一帶的元朗新墟建成。

1901年報載，有錦田村北大生圍，是錦田鄧姓祖公遺業，擁有「紅契」，繳納糧餉已200餘年。

1920年，由九龍至上水的青山道（公路）闢成後，元朗及上水一帶趨於繁盛。不過，因為中華電力公司仍未供電至新界所有地區，不少區域未有電燈，仍用火水（煤油）燈照明，要到1929年中電才供電予新界。

1923年起，華美公司的巴士往來旺角與元朗之間。

1932年，有線報稱內地惠州賊黨欲械劫元朗墟，新界實施戒嚴。

1948年，元朗已是新界最大墟市，魚米之鄉，盛產穀米，享有「新界穀倉」的美譽；亦有不少魚塘，產品有蠔、蟹、腐竹、米酒及菜蔬等。港府在錦田設農場及淡水魚試驗所。1954年起，不少農場亦改為魚塘，飼養的品種有烏頭、金山鰂、牛奶魚、鯇魚和鯉魚等。

當時，連接九龍的主要幹道為元朗大馬路（青山公路），主要交通工具為由佐敦道至元朗的16號線巴士。

1949年，設有各種遊戲及玩具攤位的遊樂場——元朗娛樂場開幕，後於1952年關閉。

繼林村至錦田的林錦公路建成後，當局於

1950年籌建由荃灣經川龍、大帽山直至元朗八鄉的荃錦公路，於1953年通車。

1950年6月，元朗開始有電話，第一部安裝於元朗商事會議事廳，第二部安裝於合益公司，每次通話收費3毫。第二批13部電話於一年後安裝。有線廣播電台麗的呼聲於1954年伸展至元朗、粉嶺及上水各區。

1951年，位於元朗大馬路的榮華酒家開張。

1952年9月，由博愛醫院主辦的「元朗和平息災萬緣勝會」一連九日通宵舉行。

1953年1月，元朗創設年宵市場，位於光華戲院旁原為木屋區之「谷亭」新廣場，此廣場稍後興建樓宇。而戰後首屆農展會則於同年2月在元朗凹頭官立小學舉行。

農曆八月十三為元朗最大的墟期，農民天未亮即肩挑背負，將牲口及農作物帶往趁墟。而採辦節日食品者亦紛紛到達，由朝至午，人潮擠聚。墟市為合益街市一帶的新墟。當年元朗有百多座農場和牧場。

1954年1月9日，元朗十年一度的太平喜醮，在原元朗娛樂場舉行，即日開壇。盛會四日三夜，包括上演粵劇神功戲，官民同樂。同年，元朗舊墟設置街燈和街喉。

1955年6月，開設於大帽山下、毗鄰石崗軍人眷屬新村的八鄉徙置區落成，開始入伙，為新界早期徙置區之一。

1956年，流浮山深灣（后海灣）蠔場的範圍約有6,000畝，大量產蠔外銷，年產60萬斤。當時養蠔業在新界已有700年歷史。

1960年代，元朗日趨繁盛。主要幹道青山道（公路）開始逐漸擴闊。同時，當局計劃將元朗由墟鎮發展為新城市。

1970年代中，港府着手將元朗及天水圍發展為新市鎮。隨着多條新幹道、鐵路及大欖隧道相繼通車，元朗連繫港九市區的交通變得十分便捷。

Introduction

Yuen Long

In 1899, the British army took over the New Territories. The ceremony was held in Tai Po on 16 April, with Sir James Lockhart, the Colonial Secretary and Sir Henry May, the Captain Superintendent of the Hong Kong Police Force as the officiating guests. (Lockhart Road and May Road on Hong Kong Island were named after them). Two days later, the British army attacked Kat Hing Wai in Kam Tin, Yuen Long and they marched in Yuen Long, Tuen Mun and other districts in the New Territories.

In the same year, the authority established Yuen Long section, under which were different subsections. The villages under the subsections included Shap Pat Heung, Kam Tin, Ping Shan, Ha Tsuen, Tuen Mun and Tai Lam Chung.

In 1900, most of the Yuen Long district was merged into new section six, including districts like San Tin, Tin Shui Wai and Lau Fau Shan.

Established in 1670, Yuen Long Hui, together with Tai Po Hui and Shek Wu Hui, were major markets in the New Territories in those days. Later, a new Yuen Long Hui, situated in the area near Hop Choi Street, was completed in 1915.

According to a newspaper report in 1901, there was an ancestral property of the Tang's Family in Tai Sang Wai in Kam Tin Village. The property had "red deeds" and the inhabitants had been paying taxes for more than 200 years.

In 1920, Yuen Long and Sheung Shui became prosperous after Castle Peak Road, travelled from Kowloon to Sheung Shui, was completed. Before the middle of 1929, the China Light Company did not provide electricity to the New Territories. Many districts were not equipped with electric lamps and had to use kerosene lamps for illumination.

Since 1923, bus services between Mong Kok and Yuen Long were provided.

In 1932, martial law was enforced in the New Territories due to a tip-off about an armed Huizhou banditry planning to rob Yuen Long.

In 1948, Yuen Long had become the largest market in the New Territories, abounding in fish, grains and rice. People often called it "the barn of the New Territories". There were also lots of fish ponds in Yuen Long, and the produce included oysters, crabs, beancurd skins, rice wine and vegetables. Farm and fresh water fish laboratory were set up in Kam Tin by the government. Since 1954, a lot of farms were converted into fish ponds, breeding flathead mullet, tilapia, milk fish, tench and carp.

In those days, the major route connecting Yuen Long and Kowloon was Castle Peak Road and the major transportation was bus route no. 16 which travelled from Jordan Road to Yuen Long.

In 1949, Yuen Long Amusement Park opened. The park offered different kinds of gaming facilities and toy booths to visitors. The park closed in 1952.

After the completion of Lam Kam Road connecting Lam Tsuen and Kam Tin, the authority planned to build Route Twisk, which travelled from Tsuen Wan, via Chuen Lung, Tai Mo Shan to Pat Heung in Yuen Long in 1950. The route was opened later in 1953.

In June 1950, telephone was introduced in Yuen Long. The first telephone was installed in the meeting room of Yuen Long Merchants' Association, while the second one in Hop Yick Company, charging 30 cents for each phone call. The second batch of 13 telephones was installed one year later. Rediffusion Radio extended its service to Yuen Long, Fanling and Sheung Shui in 1954.

In 1951, Wing Wah Restaurant opened on Castle Peak Road.

In September 1952, Pok Oi Hospital organized the Yuen Long Grand Universal Salvation Rituals which lasted for nine whole days.

In January 1953, a Lunar New Year Fair was held in Yuen Long in the "Kuk Ting" new square (formerly a squatter area), near Kwong Wah Theatre. New buildings were built in the square later. After World War II, the first Agricultural Product Exhibition was held in February in the same year in Au Tau Government Primary School, Yuen Long.

In Yuen Long, the most important market period was on 13 August of the Chinese calendar. Peasants would carry livestock and farm produce to the market for sale before sunset. Purchasers of festive food would crowd the market from morning to the afternoon. The market was a new one set up near Hop Yick Market. In those days, there were over a hundred farms and pastures in Yuen Long.

On 9 January 1954, the Da Jiu Festival (held once every ten years) was held and the altar opened on the site of the former Yuen Long Amusement Park. The festival lasted for four days and three nights, and there were Cantonese opera performances as thanksgiving to the deities. Officials and villagers both had a good time during the festival. In the same year, street lamps and water pipes were installed in Yuen Long Kau Hui.

In June 1955, Pat Heung Resettlement Area, situated under Tai Mo Shan near Shek Kong Military Settlement, was completed and ready for use. It was one of the earliest resettlement areas in the New Territories.

In 1956, oyster farms at Deep Bay (Hou Hoi Wan) in Lau Fau Shan occupied around 6,000 acres of area, with annual output of 600,000 catties, mainly for export. In those days, oyster farming had already 700 years of history in the New Territories.

In the 1960's, Yuen Long had become increasingly prosperous. Castle Peak Road was also gradually expanded to cater for traffic increase. The authority planned to convert Yuen Long into a new town.

In the mid 1970's, the government commenced the development of Yuen Long and Tin Shui Wai into new towns. The transportation of Yuen Long to and from the urban areas on Hong Kong Island and in Kowloon was greatly improved after new roads, railway, and Tai Lam Tunnel opened one after the other.

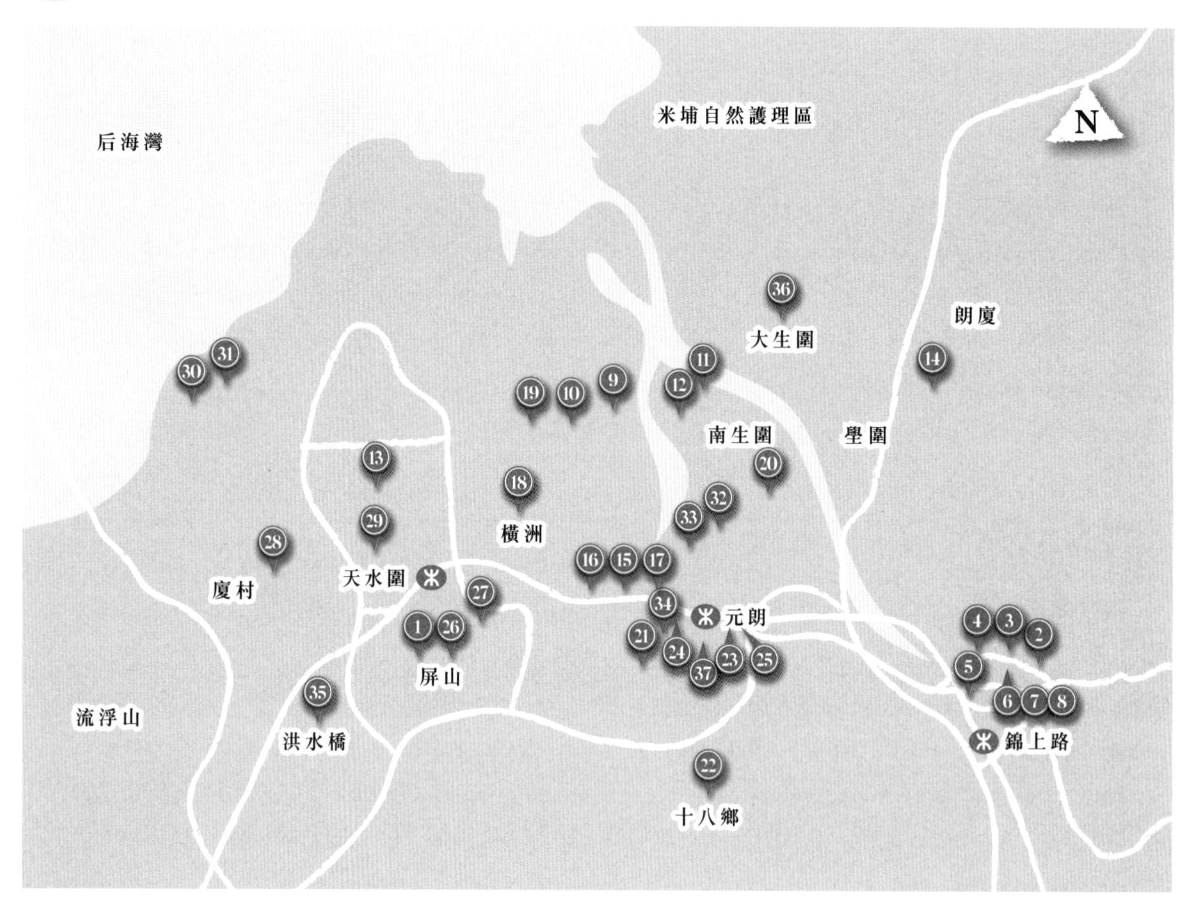

Please scan the below QR code for English map.

元朗屏山，1899 年 8 月 4 日。

當時英國剛接管新界三個多月，港督卜力（Sir Henry Arthur Blake，前中部懸劍者）到元朗屏山訪問。當時屏山轄下共有 27 個村落。屏山和錦田一樣，村民以鄧姓為主。

Hong Kong Governor Sir Henry Arthur Blake (wearing a sword) playing a visit to Ping Shan, Yuen Long on 4 August 1899. Ping Shan then comprised of 27 villages. The most important resident clan in Ping Shan was the Tang's clan, which is the same as Kam Tin.

香港淪陷時期的新界錦田，約 1942 年。

圖為經香港日軍憲兵隊檢閱的明信片，可見錦田一帶的秋收景象。

Autumn harvest in Kam Tin, the New Territories, during Japanese occupation, c. 1942.

錦田，約 1975 年。

正中為始建於明代成化年間（1465 年）的吉慶圍，圍牆則建於清初。橫亙其前方的是錦田公路。左中部是永隆圍。

Kam Tin, c. 1975. Kat Hing Wai situated at the centre was founded during the Ming Dynasty in 1465. The walls surrounding the village were re-built in the early Qing Dynasty as a protection against bandits.

昇平
慶雲生大地一帆風順樂昇平
吉曜煥中天萬里鵬程爭邁進
WALLED VILLAGE
WELCOME
GENEROUSLY
YOU
錦田吉慶圍
歡迎遊覽

沙田

大圍

錦田吉慶圍的入口，約 1965 年。

英軍於 1899 年進攻吉慶圍時，曾將圖中兩道用鐵環連結而成的鐵門作為戰利品運往英國倫敦，後於 1925 年交還。

The entrance of Kat Hing Wai, Kam Tin, c. 1965. The iron gates were shipped to London as a trophy after the village was attacked by the British troops in 1899. They were returned to Hong Kong in 1925.

錦田吉慶圍外的客家婦女，約 1970 年。

圖中可見部分婦女正在穿（串併）膠花。

Hakka women in front of Kat King Wai, c. 1970.

思成堂

沙田
大圍

1989 年 11 月，英國查理斯皇儲訪港期間，由港府官員廖本懷陪同參觀錦田圍村。

The royal visit of Prince Charles, accompanied by Hong Kong Government official, Donald Liao Poon-Huai, to Kam Tin village in November 1989.

元朗錦田的春耕，約 1952 年。

Spring sowing in Kam Tin, c. 1952.

錦田秋收，約 1965 年。

Autumn harvest in Kam Tin, c. 1965.

沙田

大圍

位於元朗南生圍至天水圍等一帶的魚塘，約 1965 年。

Fish ponds lie between Nam Sang Wai and Tin Shui Wai, c. 1965.

10 魚塘旁的草搭寮屋及飼養的「走地雞」，約 1965 年。

Fishermen's huts beside fish ponds, where free-range chickens were raised, Yuen Long, c. 1965.

11 在元朗南生圍一帶魚塘正進行「拋網」捕魚，約 1935 年。

Fishing with net in Nam Sang Wai, Yuen Long, c. 1935.

12 位於元朗魚塘的養鴨場，約 1968 年。

Duck run and fish pond in Yuen Long, c. 1968.

10 / 11 | 12

滿佈魚塘的天水圍，約 1980 年。

Fish ponds in Tin Shui Wai, c. 1980.

由新田公路旁的朗廈及壆圍一帶望向米埔自然保護區，約 1980 年。

前方為錦綉花園別墅式樓宇。左方為大生圍。這一帶曾有一個名為泰園漁村的旅遊垂釣及宴飲熱點。

Mai Po Nature Reserve Area, looking from Long Ha and Pok Wai, near San Tin Highway, c. 1980. Some of the developments of Fairview Park in Tai Sang Wai can be seen at the front.

位於南邊圍與東頭村之間的元朗舊墟，約 1950 年。

圖中可見山貝河畔的多座特色村屋。

The traditional village houses in Yuen Long Kau Hui, located between Nam Pin Wai and Tung Tau Tsuen, c. 1950.

沙田

大圍

元朗舊墟的另一景致，約 1952 年。

Another view of Yuen Long Kau Hui, c. 1952.

17 **在元朗舉行的端陽競渡，約 1935 年。**

Dragon boat race during Tuen Ng Festival in Yuen Long, c. 1935.

18 **元朗橫洲一帶的魚塘，1979 年。**

正中為南邊圍及東頭村。

Fish ponds in Wang Chau, Yuen Long. Nam Pin Wai and Tung Tau Tsuen are at the centre.

元朗魚塘，約 1970 年。

Fish ponds in Yuen Long, c. 1970.

錦田河邊的南生圍，約 1965 年。

其一如江南水鄉的景色，常吸引不少攝影愛好者到此取景。

Nam Sang Wai, lying beside Kam Tin River, c. 1965. The area has a flavour of the famous waterside district of Jiangnan in China, and was always a favourite shooting spot for local art photographers.

沙田

大圍

接近同益街市之元朗新墟熱鬧景象，約 1965 年。

這個位於合益街與合成街之間的新墟，於 1984 年連同街道全被清拆。

Yuen Long San Hui, near Tung Yick Market, c. 1965. The area (market) together with Hop Yick Street and Hop Shing Street were all levelled in 1984.

於元朗十八鄉舉辦的天后誕會景巡遊，約 1966 年農曆三月廿三。

當時由港督戴麟趾（Sir David Clive Crosbie Trench）主禮。

Tin Hau Festival parade in Shap Pat Heung, Yuen Long, c. 1966.

元朗大馬路（青山公路—元朗段），約 1965 年。

當時正舉行節慶舞龍。左方為谷亭街。右方為大棠路。可見榮華大酒家的招牌。

Festival dragon dance on Castle Peak Road, Yuen Long, c. 1965. Kuk Ting Street is on the left. Tai Tong Road is on the right.

啤酒
金行
三合

沙田

大圍

元朗大馬路上節慶舞龍的另一景致，約 1960 年。

左方「啤酒」招牌後是大棠路。

Festival celebration on Castle Peak Road, Yuen Long, c. 1960. Tai Tong Road is on the left.

25 **位於元朗大馬路與日新街交界、以老婆餅馳名的恒香餅家，2007 年。**

Hang Heung Bakery, famous for its "sweetheart cake", at the junction of Castle Peak Road and Yat Sun Street, Yuen Long, 2007.

在屏山魚塘作業的農家婦女，約 1968 年。

圖中背景可見聚星樓。

Peasant women, working in a fish pond near the famous Tsui Sing Lau Pagoda, Ping Shan, c. 1968.

沙田
大圍

27 聚星樓的近景，約 1975 年。

A closer view of Tsui Sing Lau Pagoda, c. 1975.

約 1960 年代中，於廈村舉行的十年一度建醮大會。

圖中為醮壇和迎賓處，可見三座傳統喜慶花牌。

The carnival altars with floral tribute decorations of the Da Jiu Festival, Ha Tsuen, c. mid 1960's.

29 **元朗天水圍內一座屬於廈村鄧族的傳統穀倉，1960 年代。**

（圖片由巫羽階先生提供）

A traditional barn of the Tang clans of Ha Tsuen in Tin Shui Wai, Yuen Long, 1960's.

30 **在深灣（后海灣）蠔塘採蠔的婦女，約 1970 年。**

Women working on oyster farm at Deep Bay (Hau Hoi Wan), c. 1970.

31 位於后海灣旁的流浮山警署，約 1970 年。

其下端為裕和塘酒家。筆者曾於 1971 年與多位行友由南生圍起步，經大井圍、天水圍、輞井圍，經過六小時，完成這趟「四圍走」的行程，途中飽覽多個農村及魚塘風貌，最後在裕和塘酒家品嚐生蠔，大快朵頤。

Lau Fau Shan Police Station and Yu Wo Tong Restaurant, c. 1970.

沙田
大圍

元朗一帶的農村小道，約 1935 年。

小道兩旁遍植尤加利樹。可見一名背負孩童的村婦。

A peasant woman carrying a child walking on a village road, planted with Eucalyptus trees, Yuen Long, c. 1935.

元朗鳥瞰圖，1951 年。

右上方為舊墟內的東頭村及英隆圍一帶。前方為新墟及青山公路。左前方為大棠路。

(圖片由巫羽階先生提供)

Aerial view of Yuen Long, 1951. The area around Tung Tau Tsuen and Ying Lung Wai of Kau Hui are on the upper right. Castle Peak Road in San Hui is at the front. Tai Tong Road is on the front left.

由青山公路望向元朗谷亭街，約 1950 年。

右方的木屋區稍後拆平，1953 年在此開設年宵市場。左方現為勝利牛丸店一帶所在。

（圖片由巫羽階先生提供）

Kuk Ting Street, looking from Castle Peak Road, Yuen Long, c. 1950.

洪水橋區一隊接送「搶」得之神誕「花炮」的行列，約 1965 年。

「搶花炮」是指經抽籤而獲得之紙扎神龕，在店舖或住宅供奉，以求好運。

Fa Pao (paper floral tributes) welcome parade in Hung Shui Kiu, c. 1965.

新田青山公路旁的泰園漁村及酒家，約 1968 年。

這一帶現時為住宅錦繡花園。

Tai Yuen Fishing Village and restaurant, Castle Peak Road, San Tin, c.1968. The area is where the residential estate Fairview Park situated today.

沙田

大圍

由又新街望向元朗大馬路（青山公路），約 1968 年。

Castle Peak Road, Yuen Long, looking from Yau San Street, c. 1968.

屯門

1899年，英國人將屯門併入元朗全約。

迄至1960年代，屯門普遍被稱為青山，區內的屯門山及屯門灣亦被名為青山及青山灣。1920年闢成由九龍經屯門、元朗至粉嶺的幹道亦名為青山道（公路）。

由唐代起，屯門已是屯兵守衛之地。二十世紀初，有200多名居民在舊墟居住，以捕魚耕種為業。當時青山灣一帶為主要的漁村。

1908年，當局發出在新界賣鹽的牌照。直到1930年代前有多座鹽田位於青山。

1925年，有一間具規模的青山磚窰機器製磚公司成立。

和平後的1948年，青山區最大的工廠是青山陶業公司的廠房，以及建生磚廠。還有政府所建的大化糞池，可供應全港農民所需的肥料。當時的新墟一帶，有不少稻田。

這區的名勝有青山禪院和孔夫子廟。由顯奇法師興建的青山禪院，內有杯渡禪師的古蹟。1956年的當家師是性高法師。此外，有一達德學院位於青山。

1950年代，該區有部分富人新建的別墅及房屋會接待來自市區的遊客，不少人購買青山盛產的牛奶蕉。熱門駐足景點為鹿苑酒店、建生酒家，以及位於十九咪的容龍別墅。

1954年，正籌組屯門鄉事委員會，政府當時亦計劃將青山、大埔和沙田發展為住宅區。

1955年，在青山二十二咪半附近，興建了一所精神病院，以取代位於西營盤高街的一所。

1957年2月，在青山新墟興建的屯門新市場（街市）落成，以取代原來的仁愛市場。

同年，在屯門鄉事委員會拍賣15幅官地，在其上可以興建三層高樓宇，每英呎地皮成交價為8毫至1港元。

1964年，屯門被選作衛星城市，開始填平大量魚塘及稻田。

1973年，屯門與沙田被列入新市填發展計劃，當局在青山灣一帶進行大規模填海，開始建造屯門公路，1984年公路工程全部完成。而在填海地段上的工業用地於1976年開始拍賣，初期地皮價格為每英呎200港元。

1980年代初，屯門新市鎮的多座屋邨樓宇，包括兆禧苑、蝴蝶邨及美樂花園等陸續落成。

1996年，香港嶺南學院（於1999年正名為大學）由港島司徒拔道15號遷往屯門虎地。

Tuen Mun

Tuen Mun was put under Yuen Long section since the British took over the New Territories in 1899.

Before the 1960's, Tuen Mun was commonly known as Castle Peak, and the mountain and bay there were called Castle Peak ("Tsing Shan" in Chinese) and Castle Peak Bay ("Tsing Shan Wan" in Chinese) respectively. The road, completed in 1920, which travelled from Kowloon, via Tuen Mun, Yuen Long to Fanling, was called Castle Peak Road.

Since the Tang Dynasty, Tuen Mun was already heavily guarded. In the early twentieth century, there were around 200 people living in Kau Hui, making a living by fishing and farming. The area around Castle Peak Bay was then a major fishing village.

In 1908, licenses for selling salt were issued in the New Territories. There were already several salt fields in Castle Peak before the 1930's.

In 1925, a large-scale brickyard was set up in Castle Peak.

In 1948, after World War II, the largest factories in Castle Peak were Castle Peak Ceramic Company and Keen Sing Brickworks. Septic tanks were also built by the government which supplied manure to the farms in Hong Kong. In those days, there were a lot of rice fields near San Hui.

Tourist attractions in Castle Peak included Tsing Shan Monastery and Confucius Temple. Tsing Shan Monastery was built by Master Hin Ki and there was the relics of Zen Master Pui To inside. Master Sang Ko was the butler of the monastery in 1956. Another attraction was the Ta Teh Institute.

In the 1950's, some villas and houses built by the rich people in Castle Peak would offer accommodation to tourists from the city. The tourists usually bought Chinese dwarf bananas grown in Castle Peak. Famous attractions in this area included Luk Yuen Hotel, Kin Sang Restaurant and Dragon Inn at 19th mile of Castle Peak Road.

In 1954, Tuen Mun Rural Committee was still under organization. At the same time, the government planned to developed Castle Peak, Tai Po and Sha Tin into residential areas.

In 1955, a mental hospital was built at 22.5th mile of Castle Peak Road, replacing the one on High Street, Sai Ying Pun.

In February 1957, Tuen Mun New Market was built in San Hui, replacing the former Yan Oi Market.

In 1957, 15 pieces of crown land were auctioned in Tuen Mun Rural Committee. Three-storey high buildings were allowed to be built on the land. The auction price was 80 cents to 1 dollar per square foot.

In 1964, Tuen Mun was chosen to become a satellite city and a lot of fish ponds and rice fields were levelled for future development.

In 1973, Tuen Mun and Sha Tin were included in the New Town Development Programme. The authority later carried out large-scale reclamation at Castle Peak Bay and started to build Tuen Mun Road which was completed in 1984. Industrial land obtained from reclamation was auctioned since 1976, and the price of the land at start was 200 dollars per square foot.

In the early 1980's, various kinds of housing estates including Siu Hei Court, Butterfly Estate and Melody Garden were built one after the other in Tuen Mun.

In 1996, Hong Kong Lingnan College (renamed as Hong Kong Lingnan University in 1999) moved the campus to Fu Tei, Tuen Mun from no. 15 Stubbs Road on the Hong Kong Island.

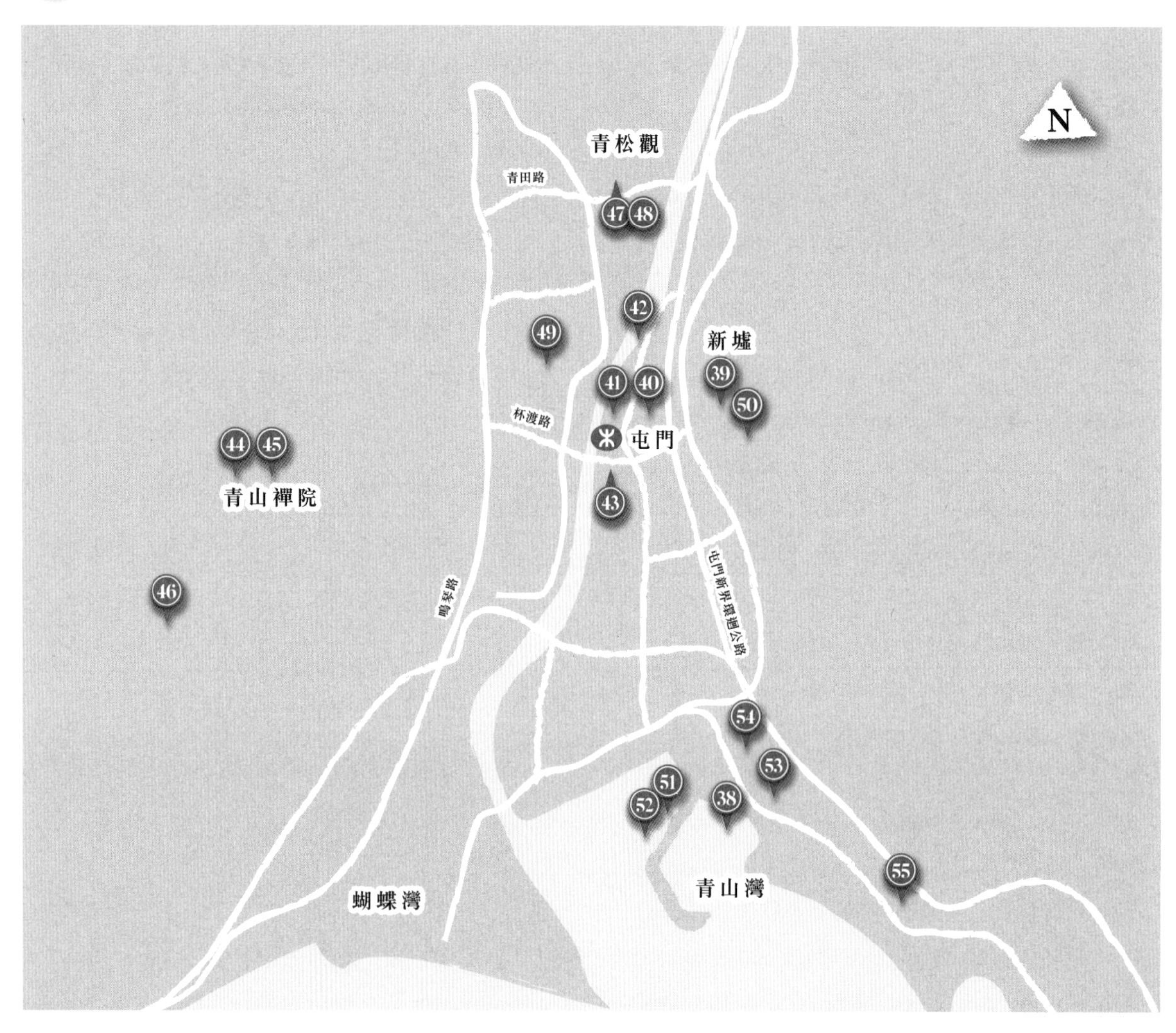

Please scan the below QR code for English map.

青山灣，1928 年。

於中部可見多座草木蓋搭的泳棚，海面有數名弄潮兒。

Castle Peak Bay, with several swimming sheds and swimmers, 1928.

屯門鄉青山的水陸居民恭祝三洲天后寶誕之神功戲戲棚及裝飾花牌，約 1960 年。

Temporary theatre with floral tributes in honour of Tin Hau (the Goddess of the sea), Castle Peak, Tuen Mun, c. 1960.

正進行填海的青山灣，1973 年。

正中橫亙的屯門河左方，是在填海地段興建的新發邨。

The reclamation of Castle Peak Bay in progress, 1973. Tuen Mun River Channel is in the middle and San Fat Estate is on its left.

約 1975 年的屯門。

正中可見在青山灣填海區內闢成的屯門河，旁邊可見於 1970 年代初落成的新發邨。

Tuen Mun, c. 1975. Tuen Mun River Channel and San Fat Estate in the Castle Park Bay reclamation area are in the middle.

沙田

大圍

正進行填海工程的青山灣，約 1975 年。

可見已部分闢成的屯門河。左上方為青山醫院及青松觀所在。右下方為三聖邨一帶。

Castle Peak Bay, c. 1975. Part of Tuen Mun River Channel has been completed. Castle Peak Hospital and Ching Chung Koon are on the upper left. Sam Shing Estate is on the bottom right.

填海大致完成的屯門，約 1984 年。

碼頭背後為兆禧苑。左方為美樂花園。背後為蝴蝶邨。右方三聖邨前的避風塘現時為青山灣海濱長廊。

Tuen Mun, c. 1984. The reclamation of Castle Peak Bay is nearly completed. Siu Hei Court is behind the ferry pier, and Melody Garden is on the left. Butterfly Estate is at the back. Sam Shing Estate is on the right next to the typhoon shelter.

青山禪院前端的牌坊，約 1960 年。

正中「香海名山」四字，乃被稱為「中國通」的金文泰爵士 (Sir Cecil Clementi) 於 1925 年至 1930 年就任港督時所題。

The archway of Tsing Shan Monastery, Tuen Mun, c. 1960.

位於屯門的青山禪院，約 1955 年。

禪院與及牌坊乃由顯奇法師於 1917 年至 1918 年間所建。

Tsing Shan Monastery, Tuen Mun, c. 1955. The temple and the archway were built by Buddhist abbot Hin Kei in 1917-18.

沙田

大圍

位於屯門青山山頂的韓陵片石亭，約 1940 年。

亭內有摹刻韓愈詩句的巨石。

（圖片由巫羽階先生提供）

A pavilion with stone carving of a poetry by Han Yu, poet of the Tang Dynasty, on Castle Peak, Tuen Mun, c. 1940.

位於青山道（公路）廿一咪半麒麟圍的青松觀牌坊，攝於 1969 年剛落成時。

The archway of Ching Chung Koon, Kei Lun Wai, Castle Peak Road, 1969.

沙田

大圍

青松觀的入口，約 1970 年。

The entrance of Ching Chung Koon, c. 1970.

位於屯門的青山陶業有限公司製造工場，約 1940 年。

（圖片由巫羽階先生提供）

A factory of Castle Peak Ceramic Company Limited, Tuen Mun, c. 1940.

位於青山道二十咪半的青山新墟的鹿苑酒店，約 1960 年。

內有園林水榭，其九曲橋旁可見正進行水上活動的遊客。

The pavilion, zigzag bridge and pool in Luk Yuen Hotel in Tuen Mun San Hui, Castle Peak Road, c. 1960.

碇泊於青山灣的太白海鮮舫，約 1962 年。

當時顧客須乘搖櫓的駁艇前往海鮮舫。

Tai Pak Floating Restaurant at Castle Peak Bay, c. 1962.

52 青山灣另一景致，約 1968 年。

前方為三聖墟。左方為容龍別墅。右方的太白海鮮舫已建有長橋連接。中間橫亙的是當時避風塘的堤壩。

Another view of Castle Peak Bay, c. 1968. Sam Shing Hui is at the front. Dragon Inn is on the left. The long bridge linking Tai Pak Floating Restaurant is on the right. The typhoon shelter is in the middle.

沙田
大圍

戰後在青山道十九咪開設的容龍別墅，約 1952 年。

容龍別墅設有食肆、園林及遊樂設施，很受郊遊人士歡迎。

Dragon Inn, opened after World War II, at 19th mile of Castle Peak Road, c. 1952.

容龍別墅，約 1958 年。

容龍別墅因設有大量泊車位，為駕車郊遊人士的熱門駐足點。

A famous scenic spot, Dragon Inn, c. 1958.

沙田

大圍

於 1949 年開業、位於青山道十七咪的園林式青山酒店，約 1960 年。

一輛房車正經過其地標式入口。這裏設有沙灘及游泳設施，亦有兒童遊樂場及餐廳。筆者於六、七十年代不時在此流連。

Castle Peak Hotel, opened in 1949, with swimming facilities and children's amusement park, at 17th mile of Castle Peak Road, c. 1960.

路線八

現代化之旅 荃灣、葵青及馬灣

Route 8

Tour on the Modernization of Tsuen Wan, Kwai Tsing and Ma Wan

前言

約400年前，即明末清初期間，已有人定居於老圍村一帶，以捕魚為生；亦有宋帝昺於1277年到淺灣（荃灣）的敍述。

荃灣早期名為「淺灣」及「全灣」，東西地界是由九華徑至青龍頭，北界為大帽山。早期荃灣的範圍亦包括屬離島的青衣和汲水門（馬灣）。英國人於1899年接管新界後，將荃灣劃入九龍全約。

因荃灣種有大量菠蘿樹，故不時引起瘧疾。二十世紀初，當地曾有一間菠蘿廠，稍後遷往堅尼地城。

早期又名「急星島」的馬灣，曾設有一個中國海關，自歸英界後改作警署。

1925年，港府為興建城門水塘，收回荃灣城門村若干間村屋的地段，部分村民被遷往錦田。上城門水塘於1935年落成，正值英皇喬治五世（King George V）登位銀禧，所以又名「銀禧水塘」。整座水塘於1937年全部建成。

1939年，因戰事影響，不少內地的工廠遷至荃灣，當時已有一間生力啤酒廠位於深井（於淪陷時期被改名為「青龍頭啤酒廠」），荃灣因而成了新界第一個工業區。

和平後的1948年，荃灣仍為農村及漁村，但隨着多座大型廠房興建，荃灣開始發展為工業區。到了1954年，有多家包括熱水瓶、紡織、搪瓷、印染、製磚及涼果醬園等工廠。當時，荃灣約有60,000人口，已有「大光明」及「荃灣」兩間戲院。

1956年，當局將荃灣鄉屬下之九華徑村併入毗鄰被劃作「新九龍」的荔枝角市區，此舉一度遭鄉民反對。

同年，因興建大欖涌水塘，被劃入水塘範圍的大欖村及關地屋村之村民，被遷往新建之大屋圍新村。

由1950年代起，位於荃灣區青山道（公路）十一咪半至十三咪半，包括汀九及麗都灣的海旁，皆為游泳勝地，有大量泳屋及別墅。

1958年6月21日，政府公佈將荃灣發展為衛星城市，工程於1964年完成。此外，又在荃灣對開名為醉酒灣的「垃圾灣」進行填海，所獲新填地定名為「葵涌」，用作工業區及興建在1972年開始運作的貨櫃碼頭區。

1961年4月，由荃灣經大帽山至錦田的荃錦公路通車。

1973年，當局着手發展青衣，第一條由葵涌至青衣的大橋落成。而葵涌及青衣於1986年9月起，成為一獨立行政的葵青區。

1977年，為拓展荃灣市區和興建地下鐵路，包括河背、海霸、葵涌及石圍角等多個舊鄉村，相繼消失或被重整，只保留作為文物的三棟屋及附近之天后廟。

1982年，地下鐵路通車至荃灣，以及屯門公路於1984年全部落成，使荃灣旋即變為一個繁華的現代化市鎮。

Introduction

Around 400 years ago, at the transition of the Ming Dynasty and Qing Dynasty, there were already people inhabited in the area around Lo Wai Village in Tsuen Wan. The villagers made their living by fishing. There was also record of Emperor Zhao Bing of the Song Dynasty visited Tsin Wan (literally means "shallow bay" in Chinese, former name of Tsuen Wan) in 1277.

Formerly called Tsin Wan and Chuen Wan, Tsuen Wan situates in an area with a boundary at Kau Wah Keng in the east, Tsing Lung Tau in the west and Tai Mo Shan in the north. In the early days, outlying islands like Tsing Yi and Kap Shui Mun (Ma Wan) were also included in Tsuen Wan. Tsuen Wan was put under Kowloon section when the British took over the New Territories in 1899.

In the past, a lot of pineapple trees were planted in Tsuen Wan which often lead to malaria in the nearby area. In the early twentieth century, there was a pineapple factory in Tsuen Wan and was later relocated in Kennedy Town on the Hong Kong Island.

A Chinese customs was once established in Ma Wan. It was later converted into a police station since Ma Wan was incorporated into the British territory.

In 1925, in order to build Shing Mun Reservoir, the government resumed part of the land of Shing Mun Village, and the villagers were later resettled to Kam Tin. Since the Upper Shing Mun Reservoir was completed in 1935 when the British celebrated the Silver Jubilee of King George V, the reservoir was also called "Jubilee Reservoir". The whole reservoir was completed in 1937.

Due to the war in 1939, a lot of mainland factories were relocated in Tsuen Wan. There was then a San Miguel Brewery (renamed as Tsing Lung Tau Brewery during Japanese occupation) in Sham Tseng. Thus, Tsuen Wan became the first industrial area in the New Territories.

Until 1948 after World War II, Tsuen Wan was still a rural district and fishing village. Later, Tsuen Wan became an industrial area since large-scale factories were set up in the district. In 1954, factories manufacturing hot water bottles, bricks, preserved fruits, soy sauce and those engaging in textiles, enamel, printing and dyeing were established in Tsuen Wan. The population of Tsuen Wan was 60,000 in the 1950's. There were already two theatres, Grand Theatre and Tsuen Wan Theatre.

In 1956, Kau Wah Keng Village, formerly under Tsuen Wan, was incorporated into the adjacent Lai Chi Kok in "New Kowloon". Villagers had protested about the change.

In the same year, people living in Tai Lam village and nearby was resettled to Tai Uk Wai Village due to land resumption for building Tai Lam Chung Reservoir.

Since the 1950's, the waterfronts at Ting Kau and Lido Beach located between 11.5th and 13.5th mile of Castle Peak Road in Tsuen Wan had been famous places for swimming. There were a lot of swimming houses and villas.

On 21 June 1958, the government announced that Tsuen Wan would be developed into a satellite city, and the development was completed in 1964. At the same time, reclamation was carried out at Gin Drinkers Bay (also known as "Lap Sap Wan"). The reclaimed land was later called Kwai Chung, where industrial area and the container terminals were built. The Kwai Chung Container Terminal opened in 1972.

Tsuen Kam Road, travelled from Tsuen Wan, via Tai Mo Shan to Kam Tin, opened in April 1961.

In 1973, the authority commenced the development of Tsing Yi, and the first bridge connecting Kwai Chung and Tsing Yi was completed. Since September 1986, Kwai Chung and Tsing Yi became an independent district, the Kwai Tsing District.

In 1977, in order to expand the Tsuen Wan city area and construct the Mass Transit Railway, old villages including Ho Pui Tsuen, Hoi Pa Village, Kwai Chung Village and Shek Wai Kok Village either disappeared or were under restructuring. Sam Tung Uk and the nearby Tin Hau Temple were the only constructions left as monuments.

The Mass Transit Railway which extended its service to Tsuen Wan in 1982, and Tuen Mun Road which was completed in 1984, had transformed Tsuen Wan into a prosperous and modernized new town.

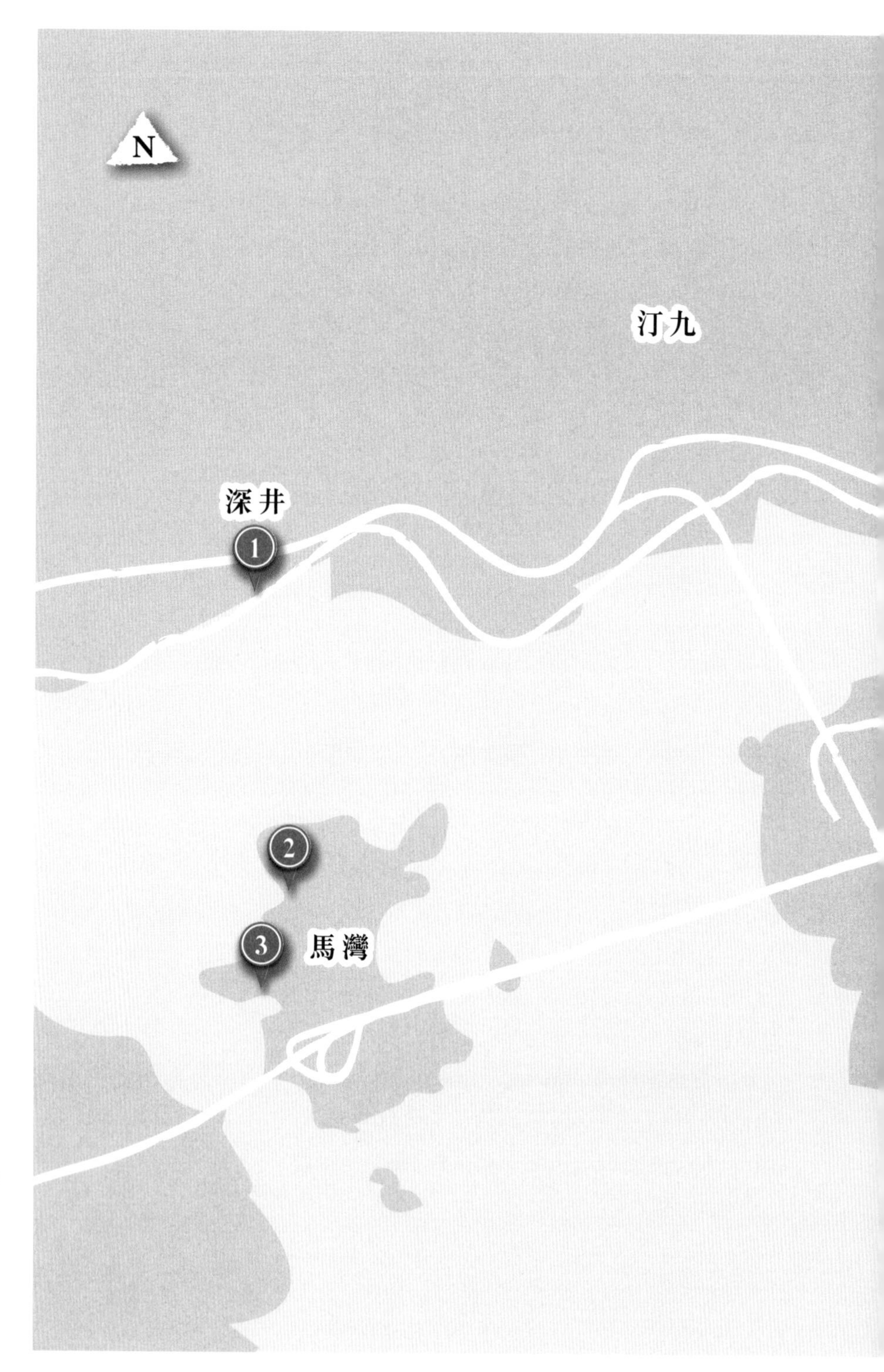

Please scan the below QR code for English map.

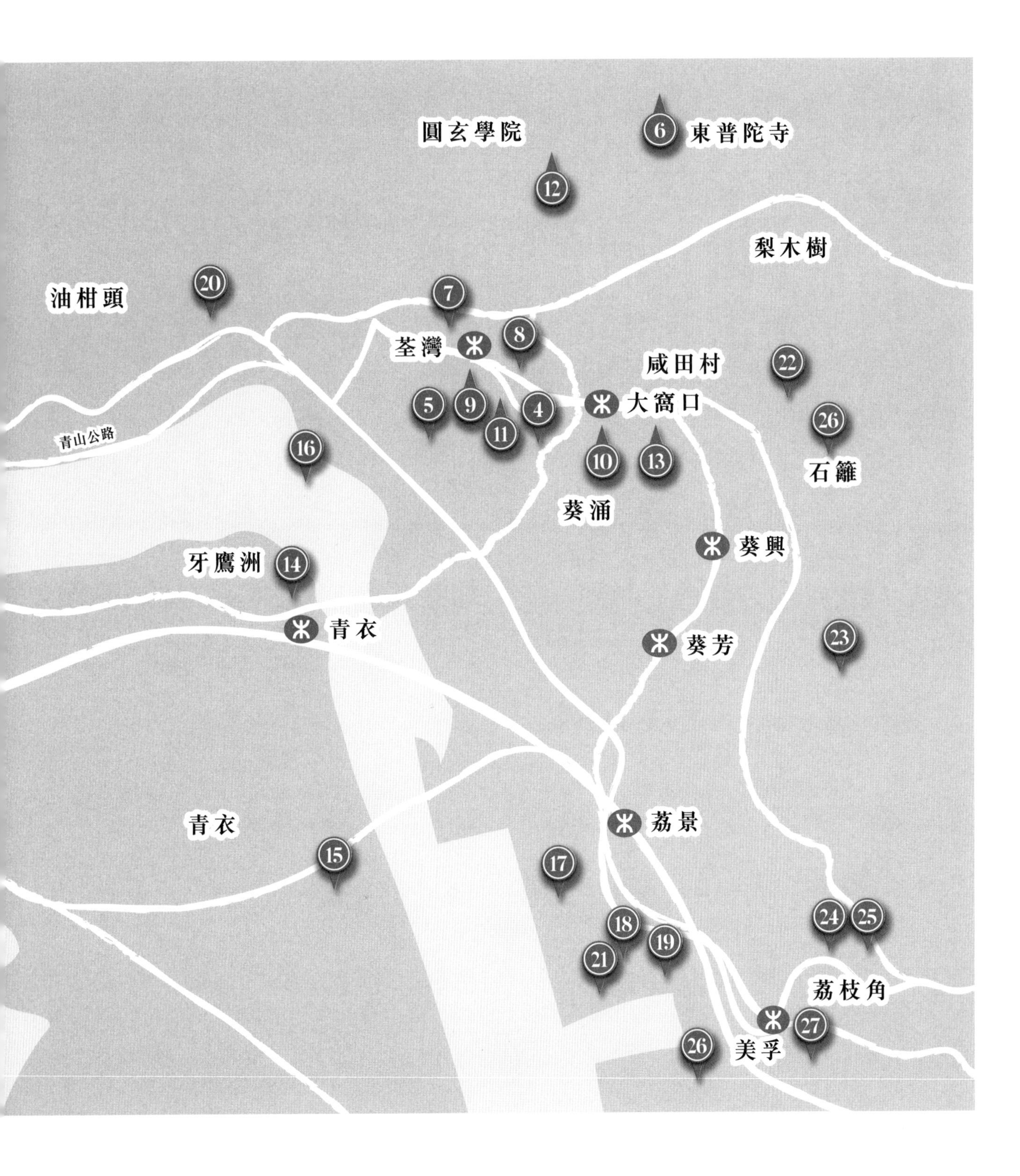
圓玄學院
東普陀寺
梨木樹
油柑頭
荃灣
咸田村
大窩口
青山公路
石籬
葵涌
牙鷹洲
葵興
青衣
葵芳
青衣
荔景
荔枝角
美孚

位於深井青山公路的生力啤酒廠，約 1966 年。

該廠原為開業於 1930 年代的香港啤酒廠，淪陷時期被改名為「青龍頭啤酒廠」。1948 年為生力啤酒廠收購而易名。1996 年，廠房被改建為住宅屋苑碧堤半島，新廠房則遷至元朗工業邨。

San Miguel Brewery on Castle Peak Road, Sham Tseng, c, 1966. The residential estate Bellagio was built on the site of the former brewery in 1996.

約 1900 年的馬灣。

右方為天后廟。左方一列前面帶有旗的房屋，為興建於 1868 年的中國海關，英佔後曾改作警署。

Ma Wan, c. 1900. Tin Hau Temple is on the right. The row of buildings on the left is the former Chinese Customs established in 1868.

馬灣全景，約 1980 年。

左邊為汲水門海峽及大嶼山。

Panoramic view of Ma Wan, c.1980. Kap Shui Mun Channel and Lantau Island are on the left.

約 1980 年的荃灣。

前中部為城門道及其右端的咸田村。正中大河道的後方為福來邨。後上方為油柑頭村。該一帶曾有一家創立於 1948 年、當時為全東南亞最大的南海紗廠。廠址約於 1990 年改建為住宅屋苑麗城花園。

Tsuen Wan, c. 1980. Shing Mun Road and Ham Tin Tsuen are at the front. Fuk Loi Estate is in the middle. Yau Kom Tau Village is at the upper back. There was then a South Sea Textile Factory situated in this area, and was rebuilt into Belvedere Garden around 1990.

沙田

大圍

近荃灣碼頭海旁一帶，約 1968 年。

The Tsuen Wan seafront, near the pier, c. 1968.

6 約 1955 年，荃灣千佛山老圍的東普陀寺。

該寺是仿照杭州市的普陀寺而建，當時是熱門遊覽景點。這座由茂峰法師於 1933 年建成的佛寺在淪陷時曾被日本人接管。

Tung Po Tor Temple in Lo Wai, Tsuen Wan, c. 1955. The temple is established in 1933.

1982 年，英國首相戴卓爾夫人訪港，參觀荃灣綠楊新邨模型時留影。

British Prime Minister Margaret Thatcher, photographed with the model of Luk Yeung Sun Chuen, Tsuen Wan, 1982.

1960 年代中的 客家圍村。

該圍村有 200 多年歷史，其外圍房屋緊密相連是用作防盜。圍村於 1981 年被列為法定古蹟，1986 年被改作三棟屋博物館。三棟屋的左上方現為荃灣港鐵站及綠楊新邨。

Sam Tung Uk Hakka walled village, Tsuen Wan, c. mid 1960's. The village was converted into Sam Tung Uk Museum in 1986. The area on the upper left of the village are where Tsuen Wan MTR Station and Luk Yeung Sun Chuen situated nowadays.

荃灣海傍，約 1898 年。

海傍一帶現為海壩街及福來邨的所在。

Tseun Wan Praya, c. 1898. This area is where Hoi Pa Street and Fuk Loi Estate situated nowadays.

荃灣，1970 年代。

前方為大窩口邨，右方為青山公路，正中為關門口街。右上方可見福來邨。

Tseun Wan, 1970's. Tai Wo Hau Estate is at the front. Kwan Mun Hau Street is in the middle. Fuk Loi Estate is on the upper left.

荃灣鄉事委員會就職典禮的慶賀花牌，約 1970 年。

The floral decoration celebrating the inauguration of Tsuen Wan Rural Committee, c. 1970.

位於荃灣老圍村圓玄學院附近的香海慈航（船廟），約 1970 年。

Heung Hoi Che Hong Temple (Ship Temple) in Lo Wai, near Yuen Yuen Institute, Tsuen Wan, c. 1970.

約 1985 年的荃灣及葵涌區。

左方晉昇工廠大廈旁是荃灣路及永基路的交匯處。右下方為華人永遠墳場。左上方為華景山莊。

Tsuen Wan district (left) and Kwai Chung district, c. 1985. The intersection of Tsuen Wan Road and Wing Kei Road is on the lower left. Chinese Permanent Cemetery is on the lower right. Wonderland Villas is on the upper left.

青衣島及荃灣，約 1970 年。

青衣右上方為牙鷹洲。右上方為荃灣德士古油庫及墳場。左上方可見大涌（現大涌道）及其右方的福來邨。

Tsing Yi Island and Tsuen Wan, c. 1970. Texaco oil tanks and the cemetery are on the upper right. Tai Chung (now Tai Chung Road) and Fuk Loi Estate are on the upper left.

沙田
大圍

約 1972 年的青衣島。

左方為中華電力發電廠。右上方為葵涌貨櫃碼頭。

Tsing Yi Island, c. 1972. The power station of China Light Company is on the left. Kwai Chung Container Terminals are on the upper right.

約 1980 年的青衣島。

左方為正在填海的牙鷹洲。中左方為長青邨。左上方可見於 1974 年落成的青衣大橋。

Tsing Yi Island, c. 1980. Nga Ying Chau (under reclamation) is on the left. Cheung Ching Estate is on the middle left. The Tsing Yi Bridge, completed in 1974, is next to it.

約 1977 年的葵涌貨櫃碼頭。

其後方為剛入伙的祖堯邨。

Kwai Chung Container Terminals, c. 1977. The just completed Cho Yiu Chuen housing estate is at the back.

沙田

大圍

1972年，剛開始營運的葵涌貨櫃碼頭。

右上方為興建中的青衣大橋。

The just operated Kwai Chung Container Terminals, 1972. Tsing Yi Bridge on the upper right is under construction.

沙田
大圍

正在開發的青衣島，約 1976 年。

可見於 1974 年落成、橫跨藍巴勒海峽的青衣大橋。大橋落成後，青衣立即成為「宜居」的市鎮。前方為葵涌貨櫃碼頭。

Kwai Chung Container Terminals and Tsing Yi Island under development, c. 1976. Tsing Yi Bridge, completed in 1974, is on the middle right.

從油柑頭一帶望向荃灣及青衣島，約 1988 年。

橫跨藍巴勒海峽的青荃橋（前）及青衣大橋落成後，青衣瞬即成為一個繁盛的市鎮。

Tsuen Wan and Tsing Yi Island, looking from Yau Kom Tau, c. 1988. Tsing Tsuen Bridge and Tsing Yi Bridge crossing Rambler Channel are both in use.

剛開業時的葵涌貨櫃碼頭，1972 年。

右上方為正着手開發的青衣島。左上方的美孚新邨已全部落成入伙。

The just operated Kwai Chung Container Terminals, 1972. Tsing Yi Island on the upper right is under development. Mei Foo Sun Chuen is on the upper left.

興建中的葵涌石籬乙類廉租屋邨，約 1970 年。

Public Housing Estates in Shek Lei, Kwai Chung, was under construction, c. 1970.

約 1951 年的青山道（公路）葵涌段。

該段路當時為往新界唯一主要道路。右中部為大窩口交匯處。左方地段現時為麗瑤邨。右方對上的山段現時建有華景山莊等屋苑。

Castle Peak Road - Kwai Chung section, looking towards Tai Wo Hau district, c. 1951. The area on the left is where Lai Yiu Estate situated today.

1950 年代中的荔枝角區。

該區於 1948 年開業的荔園遊樂場一直深受市民歡迎。左中部軍營旁的海堤後來開闢了東京街。右方的醉酒灣於 1960 年代初進行大規模填海，開闢了包括貨櫃碼頭和新葵涌區。

Lai Chi Kok district, mid 1950's. The Lai Chi Kok Amusement Park, opened in 1948, is at the front. The bay area on the right, reclaimed in the mid 1960's, are where Kwai Chung Container Terminals and the new Kwai Chung district situated today.

迎親

沙田

大圍

設於荔園遊樂場毗鄰的宋城，約 1975 年。

宋城於 1970 年代初開業，一直吸引不少外國遊客參觀。

The Sung Dynasty Village, neighbour of the Lai Chi Kok Amusement Park, c. 1975.

在荔枝角海面划艇的情侶，約 1968 年。

橫亘的荔枝角大橋於同年落成，是葵涌道一部分。右方為美孚新邨。左中部為兩座泳棚及荔園遊樂場。這一帶的海面稍後被填平成陸地。

A couple rowing boats at Lai Chi Kok Bay, under the just completed Lai Chi Kok Bridge (part of Kwai Chung Road), c. 1968. Mei Foo Sun Chuen is on the right. Two swimming sheds and Lai Chi Kok Amusement Park are on the middle left.

美孚新邨及剛落成通車的葵涌道（荔枝角大橋），約 1969 年。

Mei Foo Sun Chuen and the just completed Kwai Chung Road (Lai Chi Kok Bridge), c. 1969.

環繞新界一周的行程至此宣告完滿結束。

25 | 26
27

路線九

離島環迴遊

Route 9

Roundtrip on Outlying Islands

前言

英國人接管新界後，於1899年將大鵬灣吐露港，以及隸屬於沙頭角的離島，如塔門、東平洲及吉澳等，劃歸東島洞全約。而位於西面的離島如大嶼山、坪洲、長洲及南丫島等，則劃歸西島洞全約。離島的居民以漁業為生，而早期名為「大奚山」及「大漁山」的大嶼山，則有大量鹽田。由於島上有一座爛頭山，因此大嶼山的英文名字為「爛頭島」(Lantau Island)。

接近港島南區的南丫島，又名博寮島及舶寮洲，相傳為海盜張保仔活動之地，故有一張保仔洞。島上大部分為山段，居民不多。1909年，報載有居民偷石而被罰款的新聞。

當年，亦有報載長洲（又名「啞鈴島」）有不少教會人士建屋居住，稍後才有港九市民前往遊覽及定居。長洲東邊的東灣，適宜游泳。1912年，長洲警署被劫，三名印警殉職。

1913年，長洲電力公司成立，到了1984年，改由中華電力公司供電。

1938年，長洲已有由「方便所」擴建而成的方便醫院，以及於同年由胡文虎捐建的長洲醫院，猶如一座小城市。

長洲島上有大新街、興隆街、北社街、新興街及中興街等五條大街。1951年3月，盛大慶祝北帝誕。到了5月，舉行「迎神賽會打大醮」（太平清醮）三天，大小漁船紛紛歸帆，來往中環的渡輪開特別班次。醮會設有多座三、四丈高的包山。除飄色會景巡遊外，亦有擔抬多間廟宇的神像巡遊，之後鬥快將神像抬歸回各廟宇，此種儀式名為「走菩薩」。

1955年，長洲開始有自來水供應。

在長洲附近有一個尼姑洲。1951年，當局開始把大口環的痲瘋病患移往尼姑洲，名稱改為喜靈洲。該島有船來往坪洲。

尼姑洲旁有另一離島坪洲，早期又名「平洲」，島上有若干間火柴廠。有一個游泳場位於東灣。1951年，有居民5,000多名，當年正籌建一間醫院及消防局。著名景點有手指山及龍母廟等。

1953年10月，大嶼山梅窩完成居民戶籍登記，移居該處者須申報。梅窩屬區有涌口鄉、鹿地塘、白銀鄉及大地塘四大鄉村。梅窩的銀鑛灣為市民的游泳勝地。白銀鄉旁的銀鑛洞及瀑布為著名景點。當時，梅窩有30多間家庭式腐竹製造廠。

1954年4月，當局開發大嶼山公地，推出拍賣，每英呎底價為1仙。該等地段位於杯（貝）

澳、十塱舊村、塘福、水口、長沙及石壁一帶。1955年，當局開闢由梅窩經過包括貝澳、磡石灣等七個村落並直達長沙的大嶼山公路，全長五英里，於1957年落成。

當年，新界大澳及長洲海面盛產黃花魚，每年10月的黃花魚汛期，漁船紛紛出海，大都滿載而歸。

南丫島於1958年興築南丫環島公路，途經榕樹灣大街、大園村、橫塱村、大灣新村及舊村而至洪聖爺灣。1970年代後期，香港電燈公司在南丫島菠蘿咀興建龐大的發電廠，於1982年落成。

1963年4月，位於石鼓洲（原名石棺洲）上的戒毒所開幕。

1971年，位於大澳的新公路落成。當時大嶼山的旅遊景點為鳳凰山及昂坪的寶蓮寺。

1960年，當局曾計劃興建鐵路至荃灣，由荃灣築公路及大橋通達大嶼山，而馬灣則有一重要的中轉角色。

1969年，中華電力在青衣島的發電廠落成啟用。1970年代，由太古及黃埔船塢組成的聯合船塢亦遷至此。到了1977年，青衣已成為造船工業基地。

1980年，當局在青衣填海以發展新市鎮，亦計劃興建跨海大橋，連接青衣、馬灣以直達大嶼山，並在東涌對開之赤鱲角興建新機場。

此計劃要到1989年才開展，大嶼山新機場最終於1998年落成。

Introduction

Since the British took over the New Territories in 1899, Mirs Bay, Tolo Harbour, as well as outlying islands previously under Sha Tau Kok district, like Tap Mun, Tung Ping Chau and Kat O, were all incorporated into Tung Dou Dong section. Those outlying islands in the west, including Lantau Island, Peng Chau, Cheung Chau and Lamma Island were put under Sai Dou Dong section. People inhabited on these islands made their living by fishing. There were also a lot of salt fields on Lantau Island. The English name of Lantau Island came from the Chinese transcription of "a broken head" Island.

Lamma Island (previously called Pok Liu Chau) is situated near the Southern District on Hong Kong Island. It was said that in the past the notorious pirate Cheung Po Tsai often appeared in the area nearby and all his treasures were hidden in a "Cheung Po Tsai Cave" on the island. There were not many people on the island since it is mountainous. In 1909, a resident was fined for stealing stones.

In the same year, the newspaper reported that many people of the church built houses on Cheung Chau (also called Dumbbell Island because of its shape) to live. Later, people from Hong Kong Island and Kowloon started to travel and live there. Tung Wan, situated on the east side of Cheung Chau, was then a nice place for swimming. In 1912, the Cheung Chau police station was robbed and three Indian policemen were killed.

In 1913, Cheung Chau Electric Company was established. Electricity was later provided by China Light & Power Limited since 1984.

In 1938, there was already a Fong Pin Hospital converted from a "Fong Pin" clinic on Cheung Chau. Tycoon Mr. Aw Boon-Haw also donated to build Cheung Chau Hospital (later renamed as St. John Hospital) in the same year. Cheung Chau was like a little town since then.

Five major streets on Cheung Chau include Tai Sun Street, Hing Lung Street, Pak She Street, San Hing Street and Chung Hing Street. In March 1951, people celebrated the Pak Tai Festival. Later in May, the Da Jiu Festival was held for three days. During the festival, all fishing boats of the residents would come back to Cheung Chau, and there would be special ferry services between Cheung Chau and Central. People would set up several "bun towers" of 30 to 40 feet high and there would be "Piu Sik" parade. There would also be a ceremony called "the Bodhisattva run" in which people carried statues of different deities from various temples to the parade and then raced back to the respective temples.

In 1955, water supply commenced on Cheung Chau.

There is an island called Nai Gu (Buddhist nun) Island near Cheung Chau. In 1951, the authority started to migrate leprosy patients from Sandy Bay on the west Hong Kong Island to Nai Gu Island. The island was then renamed as Hei Ling Chau, with sea transportation to and from Peng Chau.

Peng Chau is another island next to Hei Ling Chau. There were several matches factories on the island in the past. A beach was located at Tung Wan. In 1951, more than 5,000 residents lived on the island and a hospital as well as a fire station were about to be built. Major attractions included Finger Hill and Lung Mo Temple.

In October 1953, household registry was completed in Mui Wo on Lantau Island. People moved to there had to report to the authority. Four major villages in Mui Wo include Chung Hau, Luk Tei Tong, Pak Ngan Heung and Tai Tei Tong. Silvermine Bay Beach was a perfect swimming spot. Other famous attractions included Silvermine Cave and Silvermine Waterfall. In the past, there were more than 30 small-scale beancurd skin factories in Mui Wo.

In April 1954, common land on Lantau Island was auctioned by the authority for development. The auction price started at 1 cent per square feet. The areas for auction included Pui O, Shap Long Kau Tsuen, Tong Fuk, Shui Hau, Cheung Sha and Shek Pik. In 1955, the authority constructed Lantau Road (later renamed as South Lantau Road), which was five miles long and travelled from Mui Wo, via seven villages in Pui O and San Shek Wan to Cheung Sha. The road was completed in 1957.

In the past, the sea of Tai O and Cheung Chau abounded in yellow croakers and during flood period in October every year, fishing boats would often come back with huge catch.

In 1958, a circuit road was built on Lamma Island which travelled along Yung Shue Wan

Main Street, Tai Wai Village, Wan Long Village, Tai Wan San Tsuen, Tai Wan Kau Tsuen to Hung Shing Ye Bay. In the late 1970's, Hongkong Electric Company constructed a large-scale power station in Po Lo Tsui on the island, and was completed in 1982.

In April 1963, an addiction treatment centre was opened on Shek Kwu Chau (formerly called Coffin Island).

In 1971, a new road was completed in Tai O. In those days, tourist attractions on Lantau Island included Lantau Peak and Po Lin Monastery in Ngong Ping.

In 1960, the authority had a plan to extend the railway to Tsuen Wan and to build a road and a bridge connecting Tsuen Wan and Lantau Island. Ma Wan would act as an important transition point.

The power station built by China Light Company on Tsing Yi Island was opened in 1969. In the 1970's, United Dockyards, established jointly by Taikoo Dockyard and Whampoa Dockyard, was also relocated to Tsing Yi. Tsing Yi had been a shipbuilding base since 1977.

In 1980, the authority carried out reclamation in Tsing Yi to develop a new town. A cross-sea bridge connecting Tsing Yi, Ma Wan and Lantau Island would also be built. The development programme included constructing a new international airport in Chek Lap Kok near Tung Chung.

The development programme commenced in 1989 and the new airport was finally completed in 1998.

Please scan the below QR code for English map.

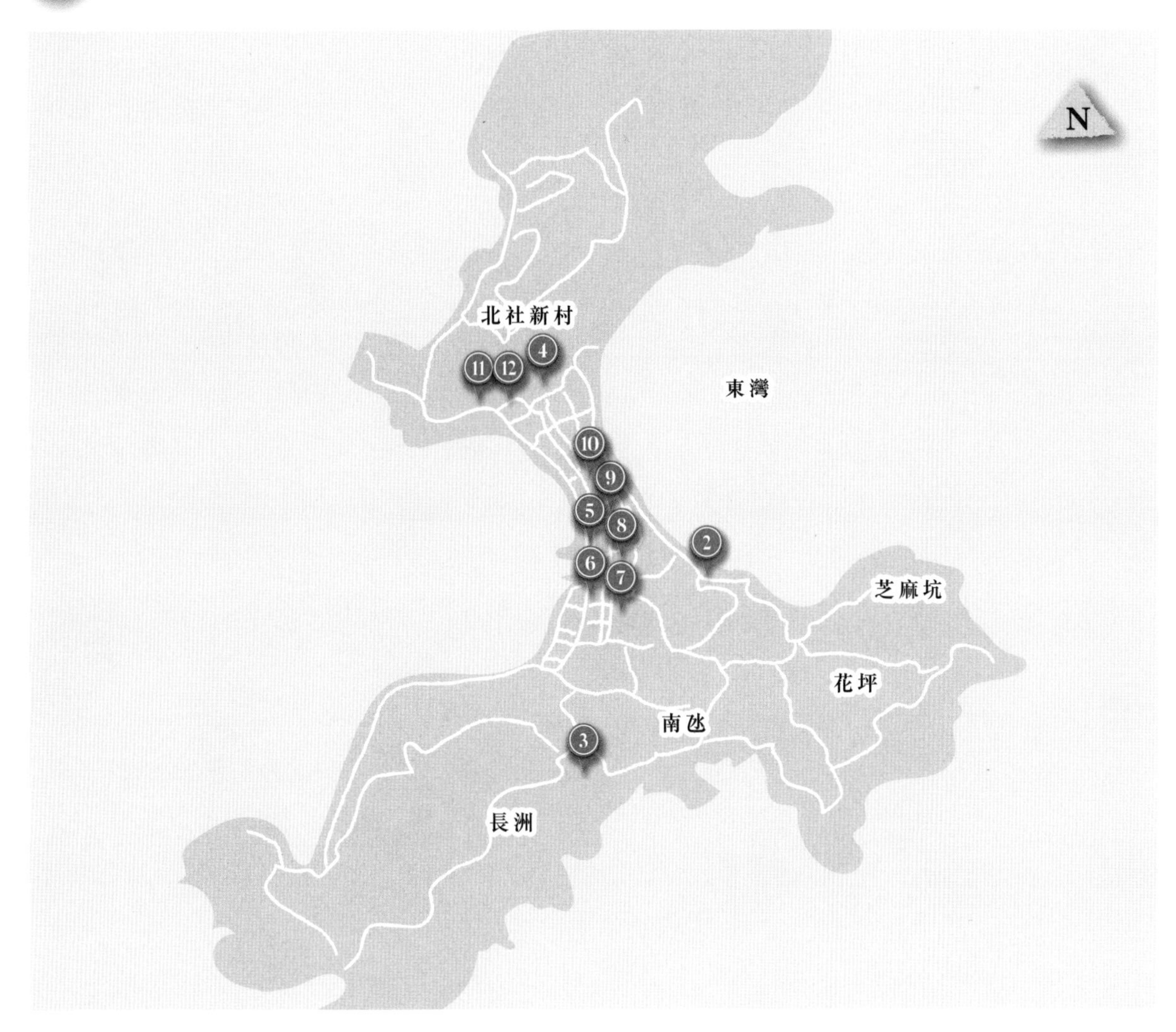

Please scan the below QR code for English map.

III
N
港珠澳大橋
香港口岸人工島
34
赤鱲角
東涌
29
30
31
32
昂坪
27
28
大澳
24
21
20
22
23
26
25
大嶼山
東涌道
大澳道
羌山道
長沙
塘福
嶼南道

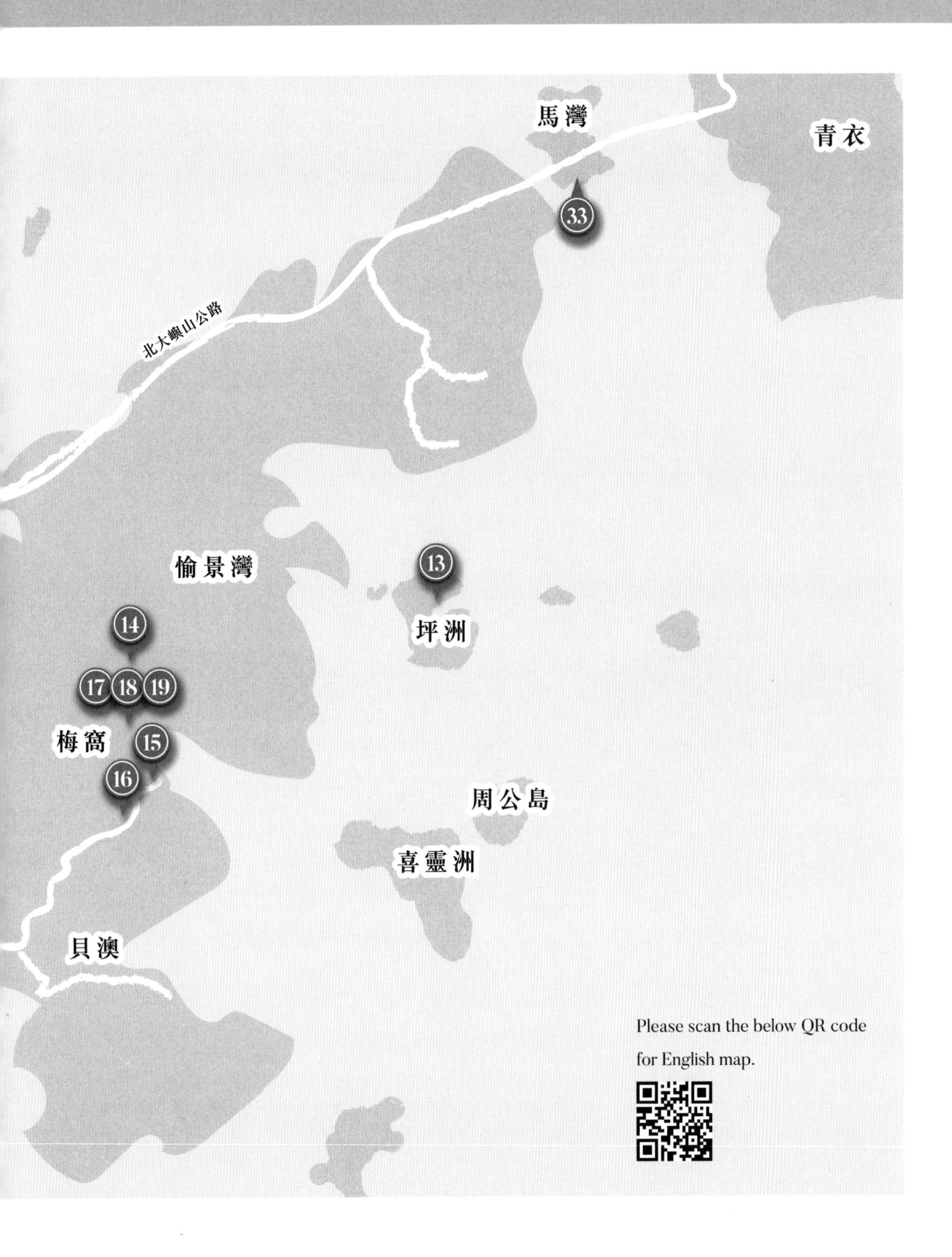
馬灣
青衣
33
北大嶼山公路
愉景灣
13
坪洲
14
17
18
19
梅窩
15
16
周公島
喜靈洲
貝澳
Please scan the below QR code
for English map.

約 1970 年，由山頂望向薄扶林區及南丫島。

前方為於兩年前落成入伙的華富邨。其左上方為火藥洲。正中為南丫島。左中部可見鴨脷洲發電廠，所在現為屋苑海怡半島。

Lamma Island and Wah Fu Estate (at the front), looking down from the Peak, c. 1970. The power station of the Hongkong Electric Company on the middle left is where the housing estate South Horizons situated today.

1920 年代中，簡樸的長洲沙灘及海旁。

此為上海商務印書館發行的明信片。

Seaside and beach on Cheung Chau Island, mid 1920's.

由長洲南部的仙人井區望向南氹、南氹灣、花坪及芝麻坑一帶，約 1930 年。

Nam Tam, Nam Tam Wan, Fa Peng and Chi Ma Hang, looking from the peak area, southern Cheung Chau, c. 1930.

4 **興建於 1783 年、位於長洲北社街的名勝玉虛宮（北帝廟），約 1925 年。**

Pak Tai Temple on Pak She Street, Cheung Chau, c. 1925. The temple was built in 1783.

5 **長洲海旁街石碼頭的觀光客，1955 年。**

可見當時的旅行袋為藤製手挽籃。右方有一間留產院。左方建築物的二樓為一家茶樓。當時著名的酒肆為何大信酒家。

Picnickers on a stone pier, in front of Praya Street, Cheung Chau, 1955.

約 1962 年的長洲。

可見一艘正在泊岸的油蔴地公司小輪。

A ferry of Hong Kong and Yaumati Ferry Company approaching Cheung Chau ferry pier, c. 1962.

大新街景色
百花亭

沙田

大圍

長洲太平清醮的舞獅儀式，約 1965 年。

Lion dance of the Cheung Chau Da Jiu Festival (or Bun Festival), c. 1965.

太平清醮巡行中鬼斧神功的飄色，約 1960 年。

"Piu Sik" Parade of the Cheung Chau Bun Festival, c. 1960.

另一精巧的飄色，約 1970 年。

"Piu Sik" Parade on Tai Sun Street, during the Cheung Chau Bun Festival, c. 1970.

7
8 | 9

10 **萬人空巷觀看長洲飄色和巡遊，約 1970 年。**

Tourists crowded the Cheung Chau "Piu Sik" Parade, c. 1970.

11 **「潮洲包」包山醮台，約 1970 年太平清醮。**

Little bun towers displayed at Cheung Chau, c. 1970.

在多座包山上「鬥搶包」的人羣，約 1975 年。

Bun tower climbing competition, c. 1975.

位於坪洲永安街、建於 1798 年的天后宮及鄉事委員會，2008 年。

兩處由渡輪碼頭步行數分鐘即可抵達。坪洲曾為工業區，早期有若干間製造火柴等產品的廠房。

Tin Hau Temple (built in 1798) and the Rural Committee on Wing On Street, Peng Chau, 2008.

約 1947 年和平後的梅窩。

右中部為銀鑛灣。左中部為銀鑛洞及瀑布公園。1960 年代中，筆者在銀鑛灣游泳完畢，多在此瀑布「沖身」，十分寫意。

Mui Wo, c. 1947. Silvermine Bay is on the middle right. Silvermine Cave and waterfall are on the middle left.

約 1970 年的梅窩碼頭。

大量遊客及遠足人士喜歡在這裏乘車或步行往大嶼山各區。筆者亦曾在圖中左端步行往貝澳，或右端經山徑步行往聖母神樂院及愉景灣。

The Mui Wo Pier, c. 1970. The starting point for picnickers to various scenic spots on Lantau Island.

在梅窩碼頭附近橫跨銀河的一座木橋，1960 年。

當年橫過此橋需於去程時繳付港幣「斗零」(5 仙)。

The wooden bridge crossing the River Silver near the Mui Wo Pier, 1960.

17 **1960 年，在梅窩瀑布附近的白銀鄉重修落成並開光的文武古廟。**

The renovated Man Mo Temple in Pak Ngan Heung, near the waterfall in Mui Wo, 1960.

18 **為文武古廟主持開光剪綵儀式的離島理民府官鍾逸傑爵士，1960 年。**

The re-opening ceremony of Man Mo Temple in Pak Ngan Heung, inaugurated by the District Officer, Sir David Akers-Jones, 1960.

離開白銀鄉文武廟，步行前往梅窩碼頭的中外賓客，1960 年。

圖中可見當時梅窩農村的風貌。

The rural scenery of Mui Wo, near Man Mo Temple in Pak Ngan Heung, 1960.

7UP
Coca-Cola

肥仔健大酒樓
7UP
歡迎閣下
遊大澳
7UP

Coca-Cola

約 1975 年的大澳。

正中可見載着遊客、拉拽繩索前進的橫水渡，當時每程需付 1 毫。背後為街市街。

Tai O River, c. 1975. A wooden ferry carrying visitors across the river is at the centre. Tai O Market Street is at the back.

1982 年的大澳。

遊客正準備登上橫水渡。（圖片由梁紹桔先生提供）

Visitors in Tai O, 1982.

落成於 1990 年代以代替橫水渡的大橋。

The modern bridge over Tai O River, completed in the 1990's, replacing the wooden ferry.

20
21 | 22

大澳的漁村棚屋，約 1985 年。

此區風景迷人，有「香港威尼斯」之美譽。

The stilt huts in Tai O water village, c. 1985.

沙田
大圍

落成於 1951 年的大澳戲院，約 1955 年。

Tai O Theatre, c. 1955. The theatre was built in 1951.

位於大嶼山大澳南大嶼郊野公園山徑旁的龍仔悟園，約 1970 年。

該園位於羌山山腰，一如江南庭園，以魚塘、亭台樓閣及九曲橋為遊人所熟知。

Lung Tsai Ng Yuen, a scenic spot besides Keung Shan Path in Tai O, Lantau Island, c. 1970. The garden is famous for its architectural style of Jiangnan gardens.

位於大澳羌山村、在 1928 年興建的靈隱寺，1971 年。

筆者當時往昂坪遠足，多會在寺內享受一頓齋菜。直到 1970 年代初，大澳開往港島的尾班船於下午 4 時開出，所以一定要準確計算行情，以免向隅。

Ling Yan Monastery, Keung Shan, Tai O, 1971. The monastery was built in 1928.

位於大嶼山昂坪彌勒山上的寶蓮禪寺，1971 年。

這座大雄寶殿於 1971 年 8 月舉行開光典禮。

Po Lin Monastery on Ngong Ping Highland, Nei Lak Shan, Lantau Island, 1971.

始建於 1986 年、位於寶蓮禪寺旁木魚峰上的天壇大佛，1993 年。

照片攝於同年 12 月 29 日舉行落成典禮之時。

The inauguration ceremony of the Tian Tan Buddha statue on Ngong Ping Highland, 29 December 1993.

沙田

大圍

於 1817 年設置、位於東涌道旁下嶺皮的東涌炮台，約 1965 年。

Cannons of Tung Chung Fort, Ha Ling Pei, c. 1965. The fort was set up in 1817.

位於炮台附近的東涌墟，1982 年。

（圖片由何其鋭先生提供）

Tung Chung Hui near Tung Chung Fort, 1982.

東涌墟內的報案中心，1982 年。

（圖片由何其鋭先生提供）

A police reporting centre in Tung Chung Hui, 1982.

29
30 | 31

香港國際機場開幕典禮
International Airport
Opening Ceremony

由東涌羅漢寺一帶望向東涌及東涌灣，1982 年。

正中的島嶼為赤鱲角。早於 1980 年已有計劃在該處興建新機場。

Tung Chung and Tung Chung Bay, looking from Lo Hon Monastery, 1982. The island appears at the centre is Chek Lap Kok, where the new Hong Kong International Airport situated today.

正進行中的青馬大橋工程，約 1994 年。

The bridge of the Lantau Link under construction, c. 1994.

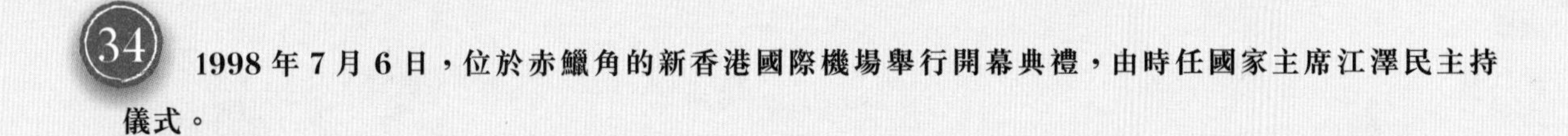

1998 年 7 月 6 日，位於赤鱲角的新香港國際機場舉行開幕典禮，由時任國家主席江澤民主持儀式。

The opening ceremony of the new Hong Kong International Airport at Chek Lap Kok, inaugurated by Jiang Zemin, President of the People's Republic of China, on 6 July 1998.

32
33 | 34

路線十

隱世迷人景點遊

Route 10

Tour on the Hidden Attractions

前言

佛堂門的天后廟位於將軍澳佛堂洲（早期名為佛頭洲）背後，佛堂門大廟灣旁的天后古廟，被稱為大廟，建於1266年宋代時期。廟後有1274年的摩崖石刻。每年農曆三月廿三天后誕，各處的漁民皆乘大小船隻前往進香參拜，油蔴地小輪船公司亦派出專船接載進香客，形成「千帆並舉」的盛大場面。筆者記得曾於1970年代初，天后誕的次日遠足經過大廟，見到滿載經燃點參神線香的竹籮堆疊如山，有數以百籮計，十分「墟冚」。

筆者在這一帶遠足時常常經過一座內灣古老漁村——布袋澳，該處有一歷史悠久的洪聖古廟，亦可在此享用價廉的海鮮。

此外，亦不時在大坳門的清水灣，以及附近名為「小清水」的銀線灣游泳。當時這一帶水清沙幼，景色怡人。

由位於銀線灣旁的將軍澳坑口鎮步經魷魚灣村，可達被稱為「小夏威夷」的井欄樹村。早於1960年代，已有不少旅行人士由飛鵝山遠足至屬於西貢區的井欄樹。

從井欄樹沿清水灣道，可往西貢半島。原名海關坳道的清水灣道，於1947年易名並大加擴建，為往清水灣一帶及西貢的要道。連接海關坳道、位於九龍城區的西貢道，亦於戰後重整為太子道東。

西貢半島一帶，於1960年代已有不少別墅，藍天配上白屋，充滿歐陸風情。熱鬧的西貢市鎮，有若干海鮮販賣艇，恍如一個水上海鮮市場，由1970年代起，市民愛往西貢品嚐價廉物美的海鮮。該一帶的景點，有海下灣的海岸公園及海洋生物保護區。在西貢海濱公園前有若干座碼頭，提供前往橋咀、鹽田仔、滘西等其他景區的渡輪服務。

Introduction

Tin Hau Temple of Joss House Bay situates behind Fat Tong Chau (formerly called Fat Tau Chau) in Tseung Kwan O. The temple, also known as Tai Miu, was built in 1266 during the Song Dynasty. A cliff inscription written in 1274 can be found at the back of the temple. During Tin Hau Festival on 23 March of the Chinese calendar each year, fishermen would travel in fishing boats to worship and burn incense sticks there. Special ferry service would also be provided by Yaumatei Ferry Company for worshippers. I remembered when I went hiking in Tai Miu the day after Tin Hau Festival, I saw more than a hundred bamboo baskets carrying incense sticks, piling up outside the temple.

When I went hiking in Sai Kung, I often passed through an old fishing village at Po Toi O, in which there was a Hung Shing Temple. People would enjoy an inexpensive seafood meal there.

In the past, I often went swimming at Clear Water Bay near Tai Au Mun and at Silverstrand (also known as "Little Clear Water Bay"). With clear water and fine sand, both beaches attracted many visitors.

Walking along Hang Hau in Tseung Kwan O situated next to Silverstrand and passing through Yau Yue Wan Village, one would arrive at Tseng Lan Shue Village (also known as "Little Hawaii"). In the 1960's, a lot of travellers went hiking from Fei Ngo Shan (Kowloon Peak) to Tseng Lan Shue in Sai King.

The Sai Kung Peninsula could be reached from Tseng Lan Shue via Clear Water Bay Road. Clear Water Bay Road (formerly called Customs Pass) was expanded in 1947 and had been a major road connecting Sai Kung and the areas along Clear Water Bay. The section of Sai Kung Road in Kowloon City, which connected Customs Pass, was restructured into Prince Edward Road East after World War II.

In the 1960's, there were a lot of European style villas located on the Sai Kung Peninsula. The Sai Kung town was very busy, bustling with lots of boats selling seafood, resembled a floating seafood market. Since the 1970's, Sai Kung had been a favourite place for people to taste inexpensive and delicious seafood dishes. The attractions in the area include Hoi Ha Wan Marine Park and the marine conservation area. The piers in front of the Sai Kung Waterfront Park provides ferry services to places like Sharp Island, Yim Tin Tsai and Kau Sai.

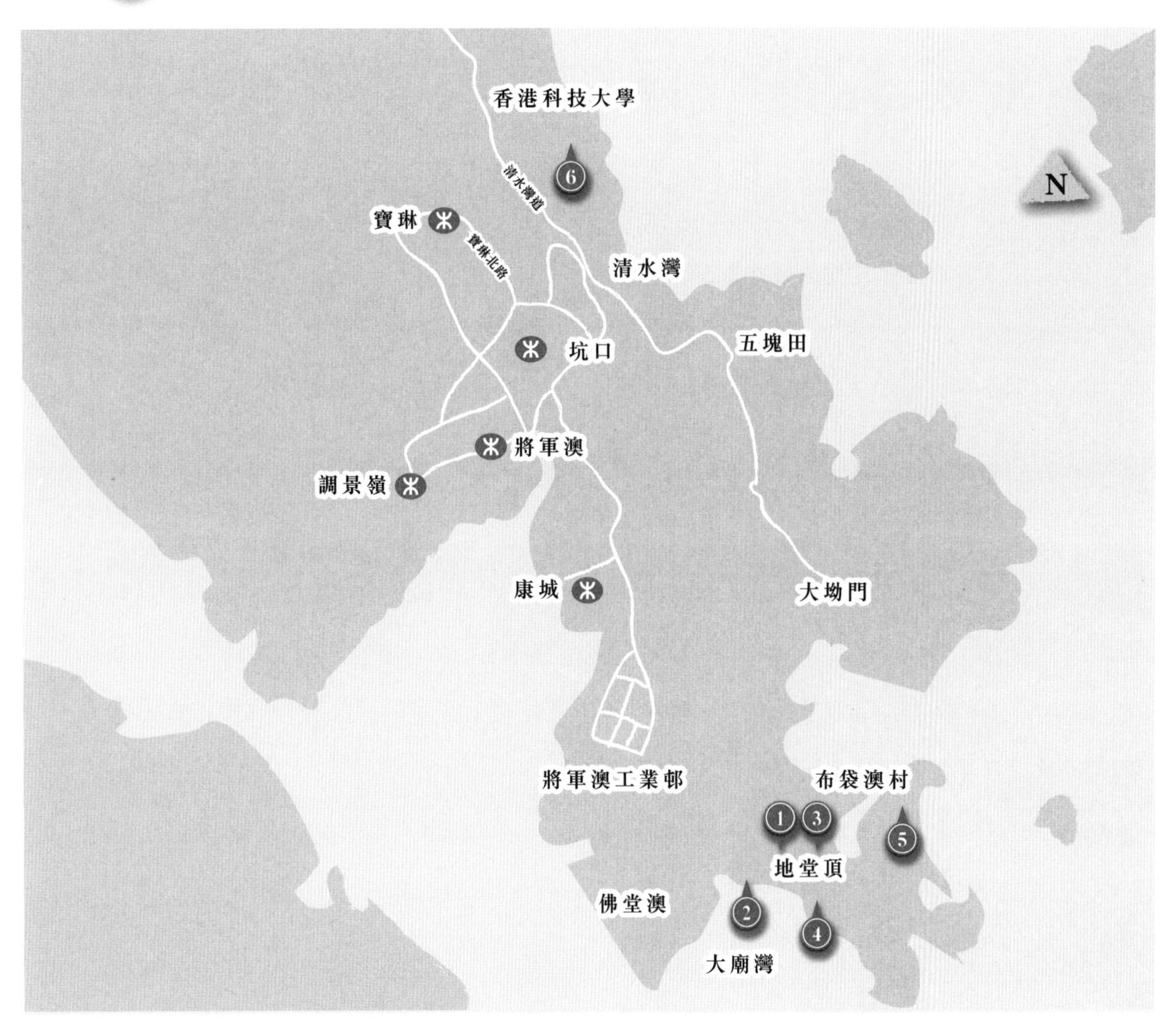

Please scan the below QR code for English map.

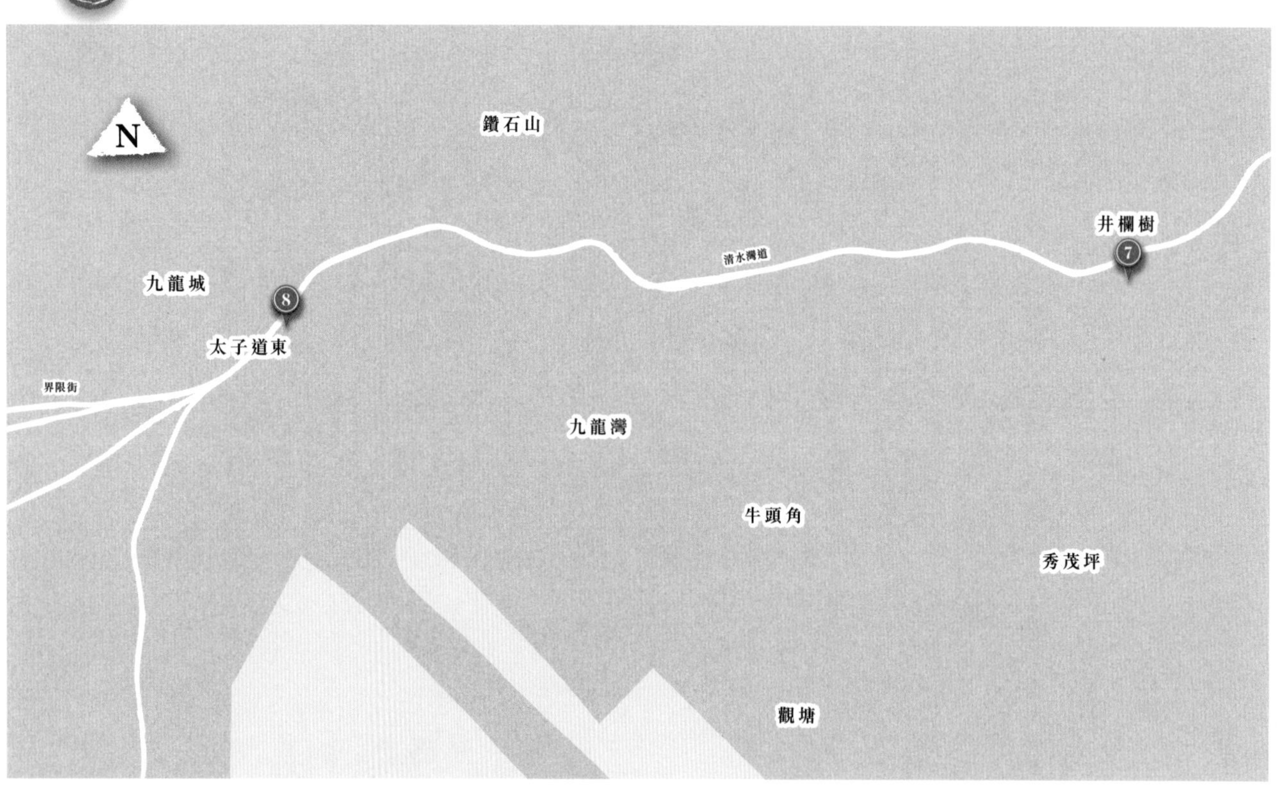

Please scan the below QR code for English map.

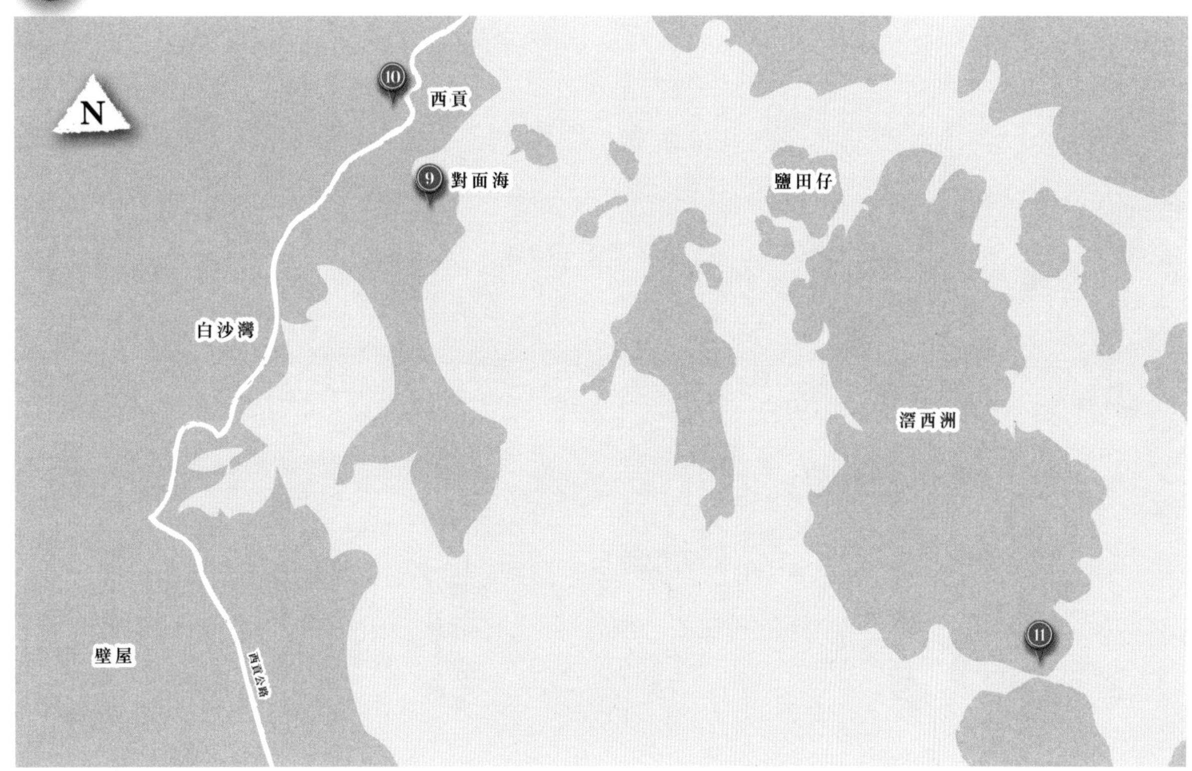

Please scan the below QR code for English map.

天后誕時大廟灣及天后廟的海陸盛況，約 1975 年。

The fishermen worshippers crowded around Tin Hau Temple in Tai Miu Wan (Joss House Bay) during Tin Hau Festival, c. 1975.

用花牌裝飾並燃放鞭炮的參神進香漁船，約 1965 年。

Tin Hau worshippers fishing boats decorated with floral tributes, c. 1965.

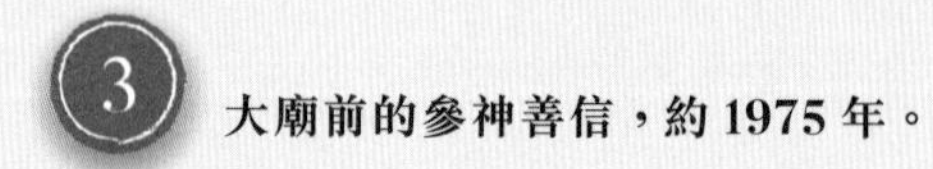

3 大廟前的參神善信，約 1975 年。

Worshippers in front of Tai Miu (Tin Hau Temple at Joss House Bay), c. 1975.

4 佛堂門天后廟前的參神信眾，約 1970 年。

Worshippers at the Tin Hau Temple, Joss House Bay, c. 1970.

沙田
大圍

位於清水灣布袋澳的魚排，約 1980 年。

Fish rafts at Po Toi O, Clear Water Bay, c. 1980.

位於清水灣半島、景色怡人的香港科技大學，約 1992 年。

The Hong Kong University of Science and Technology, looking from Ngau Mei Hoi (Port Shelter), Clear Water Bay, c. 1992.

於西貢清水灣道旁井欄樹村（「小夏威夷」）遠足的遊客，1950 年。

The picnickers crowded at "Little Hawaii" in Tseng Lan Shue Village near Clear Water Bay Road, Sai Kung, 1950.

約 1900 年的新九龍九龍城區。

前方的西貢道現為太子道東。背後為飛鵝山。右中部為海關坳道所在。

Kowloon City District in New Kowloon, c. 1900. Kowloon Peak (Fei Ngo Shan) is at the back. The Customs Pass in the middle right is where Clear Water Bay Road situated today.

由對面海一帶對出海面的漁船望向尚為漁村的西貢，約 1965 年。

Fishing village in Sai Kung, looking from Tui Min Hoi, c. 1965.

西貢區農產品展覽會入口，1962年。

The entrance of Sai Kung District Agricultural Show, 1962.

於西貢滘西洲洪聖廟前碼頭慶祝洪聖寶誕的盛況，約 1995 年。

圖中右方可見一座戲棚。

Hung Shing Temple in Kau Sai Chau, Sai Kung, during Hung Shing Festival, c. 1995.

- 香港政府憲報
- 《循環日報》
- 《華字日報》
- 《華僑日報》
- 《星島日報》
- 《華僑日報》編印：《香港年鑑》(1947-1993)

- 何其鋭先生
- 巫羽階先生
- 梁紹桔先生
- 香港歷史博物館
- 香港大學圖書館